A History of Coates Brothers

John Bernard Maurice Coates, M.A., C.B.E.
Director of Coates Brothers & Co. Ltd 1930–77
General Manager 1938–48
Managing Director 1948–70
Chairman 1956–77

A History of
COATES BROTHERS
& Company Limited

1877–1977

Eva Svensson Publisher
WESTERHAM PRESS
1977

First published in 1977 by Eva Svensson Westerham Press Ltd © J. B. M. Coates

Edited by Gillian McGregor (née Coates) from information collated by
J. B. M. Coates and others

Printed by Westerham Press Ltd on Mellotex high white matt paper

Ink supplied by Coates Brothers Inks Ltd, London
Specially mixed unique colours used throughout the book from
Coates Brothers 1880 colour specimen book

ISBN 0 903696 10 X (*casebound*)

ISBN 0 903696 09 6 (*paperback*)

Contents

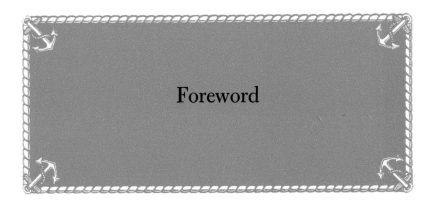

Foreword

This history has been compiled from information made available by members of the Coates family and employees of the company, amongst whom special mention for their trouble and kindness in loaning photographs should be made of the following:

Norman Coates, son of John Coates (co-founder of the company), for lending the original pen and ink sketch made by his father of Henry Coates of Clapham

Raymond Coates, youngest son of John Coates, for the loan of photographs

Dorothy McNelly, daughter of John Coates, for much information concerning the family background and the house at Streatham

The late Dr Henry Coates, a nephew of John Coates, a director of the company from 1907 to 1958, for much information concerning the company in the early 1900s

The late Bill Riches who joined the company in 1906

The late Alf Pearce who joined the company in 1910

Frank Gatward, son of Fred Gatward senior, an employee of the company 1919–66

Jim Brewster, an employee of the company 1928–75.

Other sources of information include the minutes of board meetings, the company's balance sheets and early letters and other records in the possession of my late father, Charles Maurice Coates. I am also indebted to R. S. Atterbury for his helpful suggestions concerning the format of the history, to my daughter, Gillian, for editing the text, and to my wife, Phoebe, for providing the text in typescript.

J. B. M. Coates
September 1977

Family Tree
showing those connected with the business

Henry Coat•
1775–1862

1
Henry Coate
1818–88

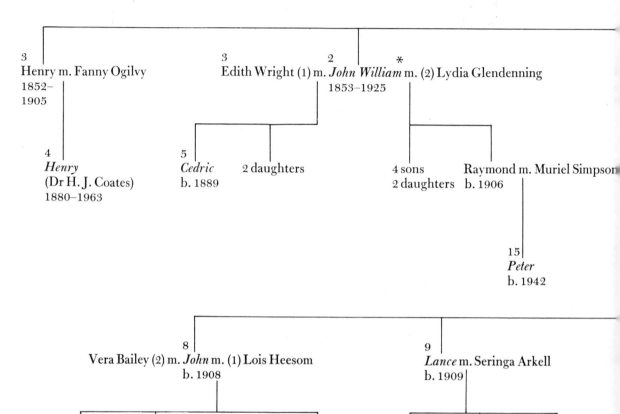

3
Henry m. Fanny Ogilvy
1852–
1905

3
Edith Wright (1) m. *John William* m. (2) Lydia Glendenning
1853–1925

2

*

4
Henry
(Dr H. J. Coates)
1880–1963

5
Cedric
b. 1889

2 daughters

4 sons
2 daughters

Raymond m. Muriel Simpson
b. 1906

15
Peter
b. 1942

8
Vera Bailey (2) m. *John* m. (1) Lois Heesom
b. 1908

9
Lance m. Seringa Arkell
b. 1909

Patricia

11
Phyllida m. *John Youngman*
b. 1941

12
Gillian

Hugh

2 daughters

13
Robin
b. 1944

ne Allan of Clapham

roline Roberts *

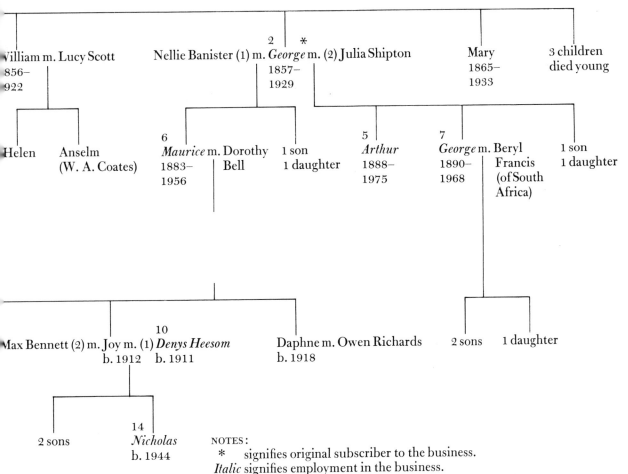

William m. Lucy Scott
856–
922

Helen   Anselm
         (W. A. Coates)

Nellie Banister (1) m. 2 *George m. (2) Julia Shipton
                    1857–
                    1929

6
Maurice m. Dorothy   1 son
1883– | Bell   1 daughter
1956

5
Arthur
1888–
1975

Mary
1865–
1933

3 children
died young

7
George m. Beryl   1 son
1890–   Francis   1 daughter
1968   (of South
        Africa)

Max Bennett (2) m. Joy m. (1) Denys Heesom
        b. 1912   b. 1911

Daphne m. Owen Richards
b. 1918

2 sons   1 daughter

2 sons   14
          Nicholas
          b. 1944

NOTES:
*   signifies original subscriber to the business.
Italic signifies employment in the business.
1.   Owner of a printing and stationery business in Clapham.
2.   Founders of Coates Brothers 1877.
3.   Original subscribers to Coates Brothers.
4.   Secretary or Director 1907–63.
5.   Apprenticed to the business 1906, but left shortly after.
6.   Chairman or Managing Director 1929–56.
7.   Chairman or Director of Coates Brothers South Africa 1936–68.
8.   Chairman or Managing Director 1948–77.
9.   Technical Director, Export Director and Deputy Chairman 1934–75.
10.   Chairman or Managing Director Coates Brothers South Africa 1936–76.
11.   Personnel and Legal Director 1976.
12.   Editor of *A History of Coates Brothers 1877–1977*.
13.   General Manager of Plates Division 1971–76.
14.   Export Manager 1973.
15.   Managing Director of Coates Brothers Singapore 1972-76,
      and Chartered Accountant, London 1977.

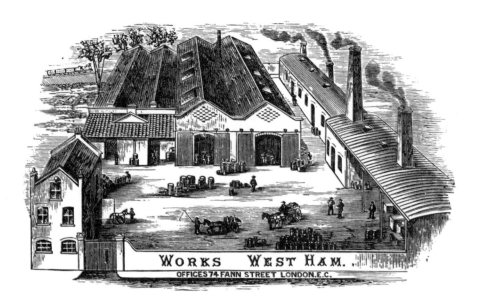

Artist's engraving of West Ham Factory about 1895. The cottage on the left was occupied for many years by Bill Warwick senior; it was demolished in 1933. The building on the right at rear was used for oil boiling

Preface
by J. B. M. Coates

It is 50 years this July (1977) since I first worked in Coates as an unpaid learner millman in the colour shop at West Ham factory during my first long vac. at Cambridge; and it is 48 years since I joined my father as a graduate trainee, after leaving Cambridge in 1929.

The year 1927 was commemorated as the 50th anniversary of the original firm. Coates was then a small private company with about 35 employees. The range of its products and its manufacturing methods had changed little since 1889, when the present limited company was first established. At that time Coates was always referred to as 'the firm'; never the 'company'. Employment was regular and there were many long service employees.

The anniversary year saw the beginning of the transformation of a small family business to today's worldwide group of companies. From then on, the growth of Coates through diversification and geographical spread has been continuous, with the sole exception of the war years (1940–45). What promoted this period of rapid growth, after a long period of quiescence? And which principles have sustained the vital management cohesion and dedication, without which no organisation can prosper?

I have no hesitation in saying that in the initial years – which, as I look back, were certainly the most difficult – one factor was outstanding: the enthusiasm and confidence in the future with which my father was able to inspire those around him – in the first place, myself and my brother, then a number of able executives, who gave their whole energies to the improvement of the company's performance. If you worked for Coates then, you soon discerned that the opportunity for expansion and by implication for your own self advancement were alike urgent and immense.

Until the death in 1929 of George Coates, my grandfather, my father was subject to severe financial restraints, which put strict limitations on improvements he thought necessary at the factory. Although after 1926 these restraints were slightly relaxed, when my father was appointed managing director in

September 1929 he had quickly to make up for lost time in re-equipping the factory, deprived for so long of the buildings and machinery necessary to enable it to maintain its market share. Hence in the short space of 12 years (1927–39) the company expanded rapidly and Coates became a technical leader in the printing ink industry, although not yet the largest company.

In July 1938, Mr Maurice (as he was affectionately known by all) suffered a minor stroke. This was so minor, initially, that it was not properly diagnosed. However, it soon became apparent that although my father had made a good recovery, he would never again be able to take his proper part in the company as its chief executive, although he continued until his death in 1956 to take a keen interest in its progress and to keep in touch with those whom he knew and had introduced into the company.

Thus it was that in 1938 I was appointed general manager and chief executive at the early age of 30, an appointment which I occupied without interruption until 1970 when I, myself, was taken ill in Zambia and had to undergo a long period of rehabilitation.

In developing the company during almost 40 years, I have been greatly assisted by the five directors who have retired over the last few years, and an able management team which grew out of the immediate post-war intake. With the growth of the company, I have tried to follow a few simple principles of management, largely derived from experience in my early years. Three such principles I have considered especially important: the need for integrating technical and commercial policies at every level; the paramount importance of developing people and giving them the opportunity to exercise their skills and responsibilities in proportion to their temperament and ability; and the absolute necessity for decentralisation.

There are other principles which are important, too, and some would question the exclusion of financial policy from my main priorities. My reply would be that, of course, a prudent financial policy is essential to the success of any business; but by itself it is of little avail. In my early days as the company's chief executive, I never believed that lack of finance was a limiting factor in the company's progress. More important as factors inhibiting growth were lack of knowledge and the scarcity of people with the right skills. Things might have been different if we had overlooked the importance of adequate profits; but this was a priority I always considered essential.

Perhaps I may be permitted to make one or two observations on my three principles. At the very beginning of my career, I realised the importance of the customer; this was the result of my father's decision to send me travelling; but I did not travel just as an observer or even to look after existing customers. In actual fact, I was given only four existing customers, one in Sheffield, two in Hull and one in Bishop Auckland. In the main I was calling on potential new customers, many of whom had never even heard of the name Coates. This was a salutary experience in the aftermath of the 1932 slump and I have never forgotten it; but I enjoyed it too, and it taught me to understand the importance and also the limitations of the true British craftsman. If his skills and critical faculties can be integrated with the empirical and scientific approach to problems, much can be achieved and quickly.

Likewise with people generally. It is just not true that the world leadership attained by British industry in the nineteenth century was achieved through the discipline of a docile labour force. Almost all industrial leaders then had started as master craftsmen, working alongside their own work people. Only later, with the growth of international commerce, the wealth it produced and the specialised division of labour which it fostered, did the situation gradually change so that the 'we' and 'they' attitude, which we know today, developed, to the disadvantage of everyone. Somehow or other this polarised attitude must be broken down and, in my humble opinion, this is much more likely to be done by decentralisation into small autonomous units, than by artificial imposition of so-called 'worker' directors, nominated by the trade unions.

Keynes remarked in his *General theory of employment interest and money*, which profoundly impressed me when I first read it in 1936, and which is the mentor of so much Government financial (but not administrative) policy today, 'decentralisation is even more important than the Victorians thought it was.' This is a sentiment with which I profoundly agree.

At an early stage in my career I realised that simplification and decentralisation of responsibility were essential in such a complex business, if only to avoid severe indigestion. Inadequate decentralisation would have meant chaos. The combination of decentralised responsibility with effective financial reporting and simplification wherever practicable has permitted the continuous growth of the company as a unified enterprise.

It is hardly an exaggeration to say that nearly all good ideas, whether new inventions or new methods of organisation, are only good in proportion to their simplicity. Unfortunately, as they develop all good ideas are apt to become more complex; but that does not excuse the often unconscious but sometimes deliberate attempts to make them seem more complicated than they are by the use of esoteric language to enhance their mystique.

In the later years of my career, I became increasingly preoccupied not only with the problems of management succession but also with the structure of the company and its future. It is sometimes said that one of the most difficult tasks in management is to change a successful company from an entrepreneurial enterprise to an organisation capable of generating its own momentum from within. Well, I am hopeful now that we at Coates have achieved just that in recent years, through the system of divisional management based on main product groups, and geographical decentralisation based on multi-factory organisations both within divisions and within defined political territories.

Thus the vision of the founders in seeking to establish a business to serve its customers, and that of their successors, who have sought to promote its growth through the individual enterprise of many different people has, I believe, been realised; and I believe, too, that this realisation and a continued willingness to meet new circumstances as they occur (though, if possible, in anticipation) is assured.

Line engraved emblem for specimen reproduction,
probably designed by John Coates for the company's
first specimen book issued about 1880

1
The family found the business

In the year 1877, two young men, inspired more by enthusiasm than by knowledge, set up a business which they called Coates Brothers. John and George Coates, sons of Henry Coates of Clapham, were respectively 24 and 20 at the time, and fully young, even for those days of expansion and opportunity, to embark on such a venture. They were, moreover, men of totally different character, with contrasting gifts and failings which very soon made their impact on the infant company.

From all accounts John, the elder of the two, was ambitious, versatile and extrovert, a talented man with a strong artistic streak. He was apparently fond of playing the organ, and kept a good instrument for his own use in his house at Streatham. He was something of an artist, as can be seen from his pen and ink sketch of his father; and words came easily to him, too, for most of the *Magazine of Music*, which he later produced – and which circulated in knowledgeable and talented circles – was in fact written by him in the early issues.

On the debit side, ill health dogged John throughout his life: rheumatic fever, contracted when he was 19, left him with a weak heart and a consequent inability to walk any great distance. Yet, despite this physical frailty, he was always travelling. He made regular trips to Germany to select and purchase lithostones from the quarries there, with such notable success that when the limited company was formed in 1889, about 20 per cent of the sales turnover was obtained from the sale of imported stones, which were then extensively used in the lithographic trade; and he travelled extensively and regularly in England, too.

John's kindly nature is on record in a personal letter to his future sister-in-law, Nellie Bannister, written the day before her twenty-first birthday, and forthcoming marriage to George in February 1878. This message of goodwill, which is written under the letterheading 'Coates Brothers, White Lead Merchants', also provides the earliest surviving reference to the business.

John Coates was reputedly extremely attractive to women, though he did not marry until he was 34, in 1887. His wife, Edith Wright, died after only three

John Coates (centre) as a young man

years of marriage, during which she had three children. After her death, John lived for a few years with his mother in Harrogate, which proved a convenient centre for visiting his customers in the north of England. In 1894, John married again; his second wife, Lydia Glendenning (1869–1940) bore him eight children, five sons and three daughters.

By contrast, George Coates was reserved in both business and private life, a man by nature cautious and financially prudent. He too married twice; and one son by each marriage was to play a key part in the company's development. Maurice, chairman and managing director between 1929 and 1947 and father of the present chairman, was the second son of his first marriage; and George, who became the first chairman of the South African company when it was set up in 1936, was the second son of his second marriage.

The father of John and George, Henry Coates (1818–88) lived in Park Road, Clapham, and was the owner of a small printing and stationery business. He was married to Caroline Roberts (1826–1909) a formidable woman who bore him six sons (of whom John and George were respectively the second and fifth) and three daughters. During the 1860s, Caroline effectively took over the

Lydia Glendenning, second wife of John Coates

Mrs John Coates (Lydia Glendenning) with her family together with grandmother, Caroline Roberts, widow of Henry Coates, and mother of John and George Coates
c.1912

'A Son's Impression'

A remarkable pen and ink sketch made by John Coates of his father, Henry Coates,
Printer and Stationer at Park Road, Clapham, 1818–88

18

management of her husband's business and she no doubt was in part responsible for John's choosing to begin his career in the printing ink industry. As a first step, in the early '70s, John joined Stoer Brothers and Coles, a small inkmaker in St Andrews Hill, EC4, a firm which was to retain its independence until the 1930s; he soon began travelling for the firm, and in due course his brother George joined the same firm, as a clerk. By 1877, the decision to go into partnership had been taken, and the brothers left Stoer Brothers to set up their own business, initially as printers' suppliers and chemical merchants and subsequently as manufacturers of printing inks and varnish.

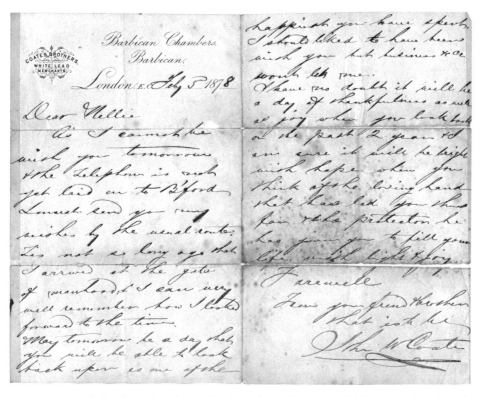

The earliest existing letterhead used by the original business. This was probably only one of several letterheads which were used according to the product being sold. The letter was written by John Coates to Nellie Bannister (mother of Charles Maurice Coates) before her marriage

J. W. Coates 1877–1906

George Coates 1877–1929

Dr H. J. Coates 1907–58

C. M. Coates 1901–56

L. Coates
1928–75

J. B. M. Coates
1929–77

Three generations of the Coates family employed in the company during its first 100 years
(dates refer to period of employment with, or as a director of, the company)

2
Early days 1877-1900

The first home of the new business was in Barbican Chambers, EC1, where John was responsible for sales and George for running the office. By 1878, enough progress had been made to justify a move to nearby Fann Street, where at No. 74 the firm took over office premises with a warehouse attached. There it was to remain for more than a decade, when a further move was made to two offices and a warehouse at No. 8, Salisbury Court, just off Fleet Street.

At the start, John and George each put £100 into their new venture. There is good reason to believe that in both cases this money was provided by their mother, who had a small private income. An additional £100 was lent by Henry, the eldest brother, and a further £100 by William, the fourth son. Ebenezer Roberts, their uncle, who owned a small sweet manufacturing business in Camberwell Green and took a close interest in his nephews' business progress in the early years, lent £200.

Thanks to John's persuasive salesmanship and astute pricing policy the business prospered, the turnover increasing from £2,327 in 1877 to more than £12,000 a mere four years later, in 1881. By 1878, the business was trading as Coates Brothers and Company. Simple manufacture had started in the newly acquired Fann Street premises, and in 1880 a small factory was established at Canning Road, West Ham, in a farm shed rented from a Mr Sewell, adjacent to Ling's Lamp Black Factory. On 1 May 1882, a partnership deed was drawn up between the two brothers; at that time John's share of the business was £2,000 and George's share was £1,500. So confident was John, particularly, in the success of the enterprise, that an 82-year lease of the West Ham factory premises was negotiated at a ground rent of £40 per annum; and between 1880 and 1882 private mortgages were negotiated between the partnership and a Mr Cheek, a Mr Quintery and, most importantly, a Mr H. P. Hawar, a man of considerable independent means who lived at Clapham and was probably a friend of the Bannister family. Hawar, who became one of the first directors of the company, provided a mortgage of £2,700, which was later doubled. Most of this

Early letterhead used in the business shortly after its incorporation as a private company

PREFACE.

THE constant and increasing demand made upon us for Specimens of our Inks has led us to prepare this Specimen Book. In submitting it, we beg to thank our Customers for the steady and ever-increasing support we have received since our establishment in 1877—a support which rendered necessary taking our Fann Street Works and Warehouses in 1880, and the additional building of our West Ham Factory in 1881, where we are again further extending our Plant and existing Machinery for our improved processes.

In this Book we call attention to several new features, among them our Lithographic Stone and Bronze Lists, Gloss Enamel Varnishes, First Quality Posting Inks, and our high-class Blacks, which are unrivalled for depth of color and lustre, as are our Lakes for brilliancy and purity of tone.

Our aim is, and has constantly been, to further the quality of our Inks, and to secure the desired working properties and uniformity required of them ; and in preparing this Book, we have shown the everyday working of our Inks on such paper as, for the various qualities, would be ordinarily used. Whilst it would be impossible to represent every grade and variety of color within its limits, we have endeavoured, as much as possible, to show the Inks that are most sought after, with their prices.

In the Printing Inks and Varnish Trade there has been of recent years a great increase of competition, but we have availed ourselves of every aid which chemical science, perfected machinery, or skilled labor, could afford. This, and the improvements we have effected, give us confidence in submitting our manufactures.

All Goods, except Litho. Stones, delivered Carriage Free throughout the United Kingdom.

Coates Bros. & Co.,

Abbey Mills, West Ham, Essex.   74, Fann Street, LONDON.

And at BIRMINGHAM, PARIS, HAMBURG, and NEW YORK.

Preface to the first specimen book printed about 1880

Coates Bros. & Co. Limited.

Printing Ink & Varnish Manufacturers.

8, Salisbury Court, LONDON, E.C.
FLEET STREET,

PLEASE ADDRESS
ALL COMMUNICATIONS
TO THE FIRM ONLY

8 SALISBURY COURT
FLEET STREET. E.C.

ABBEY MILLS
WEST HAM

ESSEX.

TRADE MARK

BRANCH
72A GEORGE ST.
MANCHESTER.

TELEGRAPHIC ADDRESS:-
INKSTONE, LONDON.

TELEPHONE Nº
HOLBORN. 388.

Feby 11th 1904

To M.

Memorandum

On February 11th 2% Dividend
Warrants were drawn for all Ordy
Shareholders, to be paid Nov. 2 1904
Mr J. W Coates endorsed his 2%
Dividend Warrant and handed it
to the Company as Security for
an Acceptance they gave him for
the same amount due Nov. 2 1904
Amount £161. 8 0

Pictorial letterhead used by the company after moving to Salisbury Court, Fleet Street, about 1895

THE
MAGAZINE OF MUSIC

and

Journal of the Musical Reform Association.

For the Student and the Million.

VOL. 1.   MARCH, 1884.   No. 1.

THE
Magazine of Music

Will be published on the first of every month,

PRICE SIXPENCE.

ANNUAL SUBSCRIPTION, 6s. 6d. POST FREE.

Each Number will contain

AN ORIGINAL PIECE OF MUSIC
BY A WELL-KNOWN COMPOSER.

ALSO,

FRONTISPIECE ENGRAVING.

Each monthly number will consist of 32 pages.

IN bringing this periodical before the public, we desire that our readers should understand our object in adding to the already somewhat large number of publications whose pages are devoted to music and musical literature. Desiring, as we do, the sympathy and co-operation of all who love and appreciate music, we think that a short statement of the intentions of the Conductors of this Magazine will be acceptable both to lovers of the art and those interested in the spread of musical education.

*   *   *   *   *   *

Primarily the *Magazine of Music* is established for the express purpose of bringing before English-speaking people, in all parts of the world, a simple and easy system of musical notation, based on sound and rational principles. This object will be always kept in view, and in those portions of the Magazine devoted to Students and the Home Circle, a constant succession of articles will appear treating on every branch of music, presented in such a manner as to be interesting and instructive, both to the more advanced student as well as the beginner. These articles will be written by men of ability, and in course of time will form an exhaustive and complete exposition of the art of music.

*   *   *   *   *   *

It is also intended that the pages of this Magazine shall contain a collection of the best music of both past and present Composers; and there will appear, from time to time, Ballads, Part Songs, Choruses from Oratorios, and compositions of a Sacred, Classical, and Popular character, for the Piano-forte and Organ. These selections will be published with Critical and Historical Notes.

*   *   *   *   *   *

Nothing is truer than that the cultivation of music invariably tends to happiness. In the words of Luther, "Music is a gift and present of God, and not of man. It drives away the devil, and makes people joyous. Through it one forgets all wrath, impurity, superciliousness, and other vices," thus the influence of music is pure and elevating, and we desire that our pages shall provide a cheap and abundant supply of high-class musical literature, printed in such a manner as to be easily understood by those of every age and class.

*   *   *   *   *   *

The Magazine, however, will not only contain music and technical instruction, but in it will be found matter for all minds and moods. Our subscribers will find a constant succession of Interesting Articles, Anecdotes, Descriptive Sketches, Biographies of Eminent Composers, Notes connected with the History of Music and Song, Musical Chat, News, Notices of Current Events, Correspondence, &c. We shall aim at variety and excellence, holding as it were a mirror before the reader, in which will be reflected the musical life of this and other lands; and critical notices of the principal concerts given in the chief cities of the world will appear as occasion demands. Music is a platform on which men of every class and profession may meet; as a means of recreation, in which all may join, it stands alone: alike rich and poor, old and young, learned and unlearned, feel its sweet influence, and in our pages we shall endeavour to provide for the instruction, edification, and amusement of all.

Our Association.

"Give me a thought, that I may live upon it."—*Goethe.*

THOUGHTS give life to the world, and our aim is to supply the reader with a *new* thought. Compared to the thoughts with which great thinkers have enriched mankind, the quota we bring is small; yet, inasmuch as it has a distinct sphere of usefulness, and will lessen the labour of those who would penetrate into the "Temple of Music," and understand its divine harmonies and melodious sounds, we would disseminate it far and wide.

In these days we hear much of "cramming," and its evil effect upon the young. The standard of education grows continually higher. A Norman noble, at the time of the Conqueror, was thought to be well educated if he could read and write; and even at the commencement of the present century it was considered no disgrace to an English gentleman if he were ignorant of many of the subjects on which all school boys in these days are expected to be well informed.

Amid this growing pressure of educational work, the thought we throw out will facilitate one branch of study—one which is, perhaps, more popular than any other. We believe the day is past in which the present staff notation may be regarded as satisfactory. We also believe that the new method herein inaugurate, modified perhaps in some slight degree as experience may dictate, but substantially the same system, will become, in the future, the established notation. To bring this about we have started "The Musical Reform Association." Commencing with a "minority of one," our numbers have increased, and we now issue this magazine, which we desire shall form the stepping stone to a wide-spread and powerful association, whose aim shall be the simplification of musical notation, and the encouragement of this beautiful and enlivening art. At present we are linked together more by mutual sympathy of purpose than by any definite code of rules. We feel, however, that the time has arrived when we should organise ourselves upon such a basis as to enable all who are interested in the study of music to join us, and take part in our work. Herein is laid down, in broad lines, our object and aim. We ask the co-operation of those who are in sympathy with our intentions, and who are also willing to devote time and energy to this matter. From such we shall be glad to receive suggestions, and we open the pages of this magazine for correspondence, in order that light may be thrown on the subject from all sides, and that we may obtain the views of those actively engaged in the spread of musical education.

The first issue of the *Magazine of Music,* edited and published by John Coates from 1884 to 1886. The magazine attracted great interest in professional musical circles, but eventually failed through lack of funds

money was left in the business in the form of debentures when the limited company was formed in 1889.

Early in 1881 John became involved as editor and publisher of the *Magazine of Music* referred to earlier, the first issue of which appeared in March 1884. It seems to have been well regarded in the musical world generally, and Dr Henry Coates, later Professor of Music at Trinity College, London, and a director of the company for many years, has recorded that John's magazine did much to establish the future Sir Edward Elgar, who was one of the first to be awarded its annual prize.

Unfortunately, the production and publishing of this magazine engaged to a great extent not only John's time but also his financial resources, both of which he could ill afford. In spite of its success, by April 1885 John had incurred debts of £3,000, of which he could meet only about £1,000. This led to trouble between the partners and affected the goodwill of the business; for many of these debts were to printers, who did not easily make the distinction between John Coates, the proprietor of the magazine, and John Coates the partner in Coates Brothers & Company. Finally, after long and difficult discussions with the firm's solicitors – Watson Sons & Room – John reluctantly agreed to abandon the magazine and to enter into a new deed of partnership with his brother, the more important provisions of which included the following:

John agreed to give his whole time and attention to the promotion of the business and for this purpose agreed to travel continuously in the north of England, Scotland and Ireland. He was to be allowed £1.2.6d expenses per day in Scotland and £1.0.0d per day in England. Any sales commission he earned was to be earmarked for the gradual liquidation of the magazine's debts, and until these debts were liquidated, his income from the business was to be limited to £5 per week.

From 1883 onwards, the business expanded only very slowly, and John never really recovered from the debts which he incurred from this interesting but injudicious adventure. On 8 January 1889, the business was reconstituted as a private limited company, under the name Coates Brothers and Company Ltd; this company (which is still the parent company in its original form) has traded without interruption ever since. Its capitalisation in 1889 was as follows:

1,700 £10 ordinary shares, divided equally between John and George Coates, except for six founder shares
300 £10 7% first preference shares
200 £50 7% debentures.

It seems likely that the formation of the limited company was John's idea, his aim being to secure extra money for the development of the business, and to relieve himself of his own debts. This scheme was temporarily successful, in that the partnership was able to sell to the limited company the business as a going concern for £17,000, all in the form of ordinary shares. It was also to John's

BALAN(

Dr.   LIABILITIES.

	£	s.	d.
To Trade Creditors on Open Accounts	1,661	5	10
„ „ viz., Bills Payable	2,379	11	0
Schedule A	4,040	16	10
To Mortgage Creditors ... ... „			
To Capital Account :—			
Mr. John William Coates	2,000	0	0
Mr. George Coates	1,500	0	0
	3,500	0	0

We have carefully examined the Books of Messrs. COATES BROS., and have extracted
of the Open Accounts, which agree with the Balance Sheet and with the
Schedules of Assets and Liabilities, and we certify the same to be correct.

Hardu

Accountan

The earliest surviving
balance sheet; this
document was drawn up
to form the basis of a
formal deed of partnership
between the two founders
John and George Coates

ATES BROS. & CO.,

OF ABBEY MILLS, WEST HAM;

74, FANN STREET, E.C.;

AND AT BIRMINGHAM;

Printing Ink, Varnish and Colour Manufacturers.

EET, 1st MAY, 1882.

ASSETS.   Cr.

d.				£	s.	d.	£	s.	d.
		By Cash at Bank		40	0	0			
		,, ,, Birmingham Branch		5	2	0			
				45	2	0	45	2	0
10		By Stock of Stationery					45	10	0
0		By Stock-in-Trade at 74, Fann Street		714	14	2			
		,, ,, Abbey Mills, West Ham		862	18	11			
		,, ,, Birmingham		113	7	11			
		Schedule B ...		1,691	1	0	1,691	1	0
		By Outstanding Book Debts ... ... Schedule C ...					3,217	10	1
0		By Valuation of Factory at West Ham					2,500	0	0
		By Valuation of Working Plant and Machinery at West Ham ... ... Schedule D ...					1,641	13	9
10							£9,140	16	10

ces

ing

Kennett

Auditor

Patterns used to show colours from
two early sample books

advantage that, with the formation of the limited company, the deed of partnership was automatically dissolved, thus relieving him of the undertakings given to his brother only a few years earlier.

The first directors of the company were John and George Coates, Ebenezer Roberts, Henry Hawar, A. S. Wright (who was the brother of John's first wife, Edith) and a certain Charles Wilkes. A. S. Wright was secretary of the company until 1907, and his son is still a shareholder today. Ebenezer Roberts became the first chairman, George was appointed managing director for life, and John was made a life director; as in the past, the latter continued to be active in a sales capacity, but continued to develop extensive outside interests so that by no means all his time was devoted to the company.

In 1888, before the business became a limited company, sales turnover was £13,657, and showed only a small improvement on the early years. Further difficulties arose when John moved to his mother's house in Harrogate after his wife's death in 1890 and for several years little progress was made; but after 1892 business improved, helped by the introductions provided by John for H. C. Bolton, previously a clerk in the London office and by now a salesman attached to the Manchester depot. In 1894, after remarrying, John returned to live in the south of England, at Streatham: some years earlier George, who had been living in Stockport, had also moved south, to Buckhurst Hill in Essex, where he was to live for the rest of his life. (While living in the north of England, between 1885–89, George had established the Manchester depot at 72a George Street, Manchester.)

Now re-established in the south and re-invigorated by his recent marriage, John once again turned his attention to outside activities; this time his plan was to build good class flats in Streatham to let to members of the rising middle class, currently following fashion by moving out to the suburbs. It was for him a stroke of luck that in the late '90s the company was doing very well, and he had the opportunity to borrow more and more money on the security of his shares in the business to finance his property developments; at the same time George, too, slackened his grip following a serious illness which incapacitated him for many months. Thus it was that much of the administration was left in the hands of Morris, who proved himself to be an extremely capable clerk. The management control of the business thus seems to have slipped considerably during these years, although a tight financial control was always maintained through the directors' meetings.

The laissez faire attitude of the founders at this juncture appears to have been contagious. Perhaps because they felt themselves to be inadequately rewarded for their efforts (although Morris had become a small shareholder when the limited company was formed) Morris and Bolton left the company's employ on 28 August 1900 without any warning, to establish their own business as Morris and Bolton Ltd – the forerunner of the present Lorilleux and Bolton Ltd. They were joined shortly afterwards by the company's only qualified inkmaker, a man called Coward, who had been in charge of the West Ham factory and who left with all the company's recipes. This disaster nearly proved fatal. The future for the company looked grim, indeed, and the two founders, at times personally antagonistic, had come close to losing heart. But two factors saved the day: the loyalty of two employees and the timely arrival on the scene of George's son Maurice.

Virginia House, Buckhurst Hill, home of George Coates from 1889 until his death in 1929

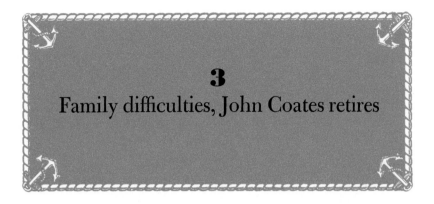

3
Family difficulties, John Coates retires

Fred Gatward joined the company in 1885 as a warehouseman at Fann Street, where he was responsible for the skilled task of splitting and 'dressing' litho stones. He was one of two loyal employees in a position of seniority and trust who remained with the company after the defection of Morris and Bolton in 1900, to be followed shortly afterwards by Coward then works manager of the West Ham factory. After the demoralising departure of Coward, Fred Gatward took over his responsibilities at the West Ham factory and held the staff together. Fred was to remain in the position he filled so opportunely until he died in 1929; and his three sons, Fred, Frank and Percy, who all joined the company at an early age, were likewise to remain until their own retirement. The other employee was W. J. Hart, at that time a young traveller, to whom the sudden departure of H. C. Bolton came as a God-given opportunity: with encouragement from George and increasing experience, he proved a most effective salesman and in time took over many of the accounts in the north of England previously worked by Bolton or by John himself.

Problems remained, however, for these changes and the development of John's external interests led to an unfortunate estrangement between the two founders of the business. John became increasingly determined to pursue his property ventures and independent financial activities, while George grew so excessively cautious financially within the company that he did his utmost to prevent any expenditure at all on improved plant or equipment; this obsessive economy persisted until his death.

It was a fortunate day for the company, therefore, when early in 1901 George Coates's second son, Maurice, joined its staff at the age of 17. Maurice was enthusiastic and energetic and quite different in temperament from his father. He quickly set about trying to repair the company's fortunes, but there were still difficulties ahead. In 1903 his half brother Arthur, another son of George, was brought into the company, a move which led to personal pressures so great that eventually Maurice informed his father that he intended to emigrate to New Zealand to join his elder brother, Eustace. George, fearing the collapse of the business around him and believing that Maurice alone had qualities which might save the company, arranged matters so that it was Arthur who left, while Maurice remained.

Besides Maurice, one other of George's five sons was to play an important part in the development of the business overseas. George Coates (half brother of Maurice) emigrated and after spending some years in New Zealand and Queensland, had finally settled in South Africa where he had established his own sugar estate, 150 miles south of Durban. After the First World War, he was appointed agent for the company's products in South Africa and successfully established a regular trade in news ink and litho inks with a number of important users. This trade was transferred to the South African company when it was established in 1936, with George as its first chairman. In 1933 George had come to live in Durban following his appointment as secretary of the South Africa Sugar Growers' Association, in which capacity he was the principal link between the sugar industry and the government in the negotiation of prices and the promotion of exports. He retired from this appointment in 1955 and went to live in Pietermaritsburg; but he remained a director of Coates Brothers (S.A.) Pty Ltd and was chairman when he died in 1968.

George Coates senior always took an active interest in the company's progress, even though in later years he left most of the management to Maurice. He visited the West Ham factory regularly twice weekly, and the London office at least once a week; he retained the appointment of managing director until his death in 1929.

Meanwhile, John was working on his own with characteristic energy building spacious flats which let readily at a satisfactory profit. These developments were financed through private borrowings on his shares in the company and through bank loans secured on the properties. John owned a large and prestigious house in Streatham but in time his ambitions outran his financial prudence. By 1906, his position had become so tenuous that the Lloyd George Land Act, which set out to tax profits on land values arising from building development, came as a body blow: the end came when his bankers withdrew their support so that he was unable to satisfy his creditors, and one day he came home to tell his family that he might have to face the bankruptcy court.

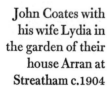

John Coates with his wife Lydia in the garden of their house Arran at Streatham c.1904

32

Arran, the home of John Coates in Streatham, after his second marriage, from 1892 until 1906

John Coates and his second wife, Lydia Glendenning (seated right), with their family c.1920

Once again, albeit in crisis, John's energy served him well. He and his large family immediately moved into two flats (ironically, in one of his own developments) and proceeded to look after themselves. His large house, Arran, was put up for sale, the gardener and three maids were paid off, his daughters took over the household work and the whole family turned to each evening for one huge wash-up.

Fortunately, a few of the properties and a small number of the company's shares were in the ownership of his wife, so the family was not entirely destitute. Moreover, George was very good to his brother in his misfortune. The directors paid an allowance to Lydia Coates for the support of the family, which was continued until John's death in 1925, and subsequently became a pension for his widow until her death in 1940. John's family in general showed great resourcefulness during these difficult times: his eldest son, Cedric, started work for the company in 1905, while his second son obtained a choirboy's scholarship to the City of London Music School, and subsequently emigrated to Canada.

John's eventual bankruptcy led to his resignation as a director in December 1906 and thereafter he had no connection with the company's affairs. Despite his increasing independence in recent years, his departure was a serious loss. Nearly all new ideas and much of the customer goodwill arose from John's fertile imagination and persuasive tongue. On his departure, Maurice was appointed a director at the age of 23, his salary being increased from £120 to £200 per annum: since joining the company at the age of 17 he had applied himself with energy and determination and by this time had proved his worth to both George and John.

Meanwhile, George was looking for new talent to strengthen the board. His choice fell upon a Colonel Hain (uncle of one Robert Brown of Edinburgh who is still a shareholder in the company), who was appointed a director in 1905 and was soon elected chairman. It has not been possible to ascertain the connection between Colonel Hain and the Coates family. He resigned from the board in January 1908 for reasons unspecified, but was reappointed in 1913 and remained chairman until his death in 1932.

In 1916, the company's London office moved from its premises at 8 Salisbury Court to St Bride's House, close by in Salisbury Square, EC4. Slowly, from now on, its flagging fortunes began to revive, thanks to Maurice (who by now had started travelling Northern Ireland, and had earlier taken charge of the lithostone business) and to W. J. Hart, who was proving an ever more successful traveller in the north of England.

W. J. Hart was clearly very well regarded by George, who in 1906 negotiated a five-year contract to secure his services. It appears that he brought the company much good trade and some notoriety: as recently as the 1950s, the present chairman was told peremptorily by one of the older directors of a very large potential customer that his company would never do business with Coates

34

Brothers because of an 'incident' with Mr Hart in 1907. Nor could he be persuaded to let byegones be byegones: even all those years afterwards, the memory of W. J. Hart's unspecified misdemeanour still rankled.

In other companies, too, Hart created a lasting impression, although fortunately none so unfavourable. He was remembered often as a distinguished gentleman in a frock coat and top hat, who called regularly and, in his prosperous days, arrived in a carriage; and in general he appears to have built himself a powerful reputation as an effective salesman with a strong personality. A fascinating series of letters between a slightly testy Hart and George Coates survives: clearly Hart was something of a prima donna among travellers, as this excerpt from one of his letters shows: 'I am going to Liverpool tomorrow for the week, and I must ask you to forward my cheque. It is most unreasonable to say I must not start on any more journeys until I "have come to a decision on this point", as you are directly going against the terms of the agreement, wherein it is stated I must travel the towns and cities not less than four times a year, and it is left to my own discretion when to call . . . Please send my cheque for the 1¼ per cent discount . . .'

About now, Maurice, as his uncle John had before him, applied himself to the import and sale of litho-stones. He made several journeys to Italy for the selection of these stones but although directed by his father to develop this trade and despite the success he achieved he never felt it had a future, for zinc plates were already being introduced and soon began to restrict the market for litho-stones.

One of the last services which John did for the company was successfully to insist upon the purchase and installation of a gas engine to replace the old steam engine driving the mills. In April 1905, a new gas engine was purchased from Andrews of Stockport for £612, and in June 1905 a new engine house and engine bed were built for £120. This engine and a later Crossley engine were the prime movers employed to drive all the mills until after George's death; in 1930 Maurice used part of the company's accumulated reserves to instal electricity, then available at cheap rates from the West Ham Corporation.

Pattern used to show colours for a specimen book c.1920

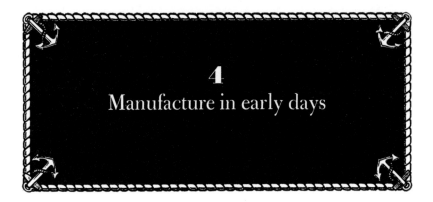

4
Manufacture in early days

The manufacture of printing ink in the '80s and '90s was still an empirical art. Letterpress inks, including newsprint inks, were made from lamp black, ground into mineral oil fortified with rosin oil. The paint and printing ink industries then employed so-called oil boilers, who were true craftsmen in the old tradition. Rosin oil was made by cooking gum rosin (rosin colophony) into mineral oil in a large pot over a coal furnace, and was an essential ingredient, especially in rotary black inks, to give the necessary flow characteristics.

So-called lamp black and sometimes vegetable black were made in Ling's Black Factory adjacent to the company's factory at West Ham, by burning oil or vegetable residue. The process was unsophisticated, to say the least. The soot rose into the air and collected upon the walls of tall buildings, which were about 30 ft high without any windows. The walls were then scraped down with long iron scrapers and the black packed in hessian sacks, for despatch mainly to inkmakers. The present chairman recalls that when he first worked in the factory in 1927, lamp black for news ink manufacture was delivered by Ling's men who were 'literally as black as soot, with just the red rims and whites of their eyes standing out against their black faces.'

After the First World War, the manufacture of blacks in England by burning was gradually killed by the import of gas black (known as carbon black in the trade) from the United States. Coates Brothers was one of the last customers for Ling's Black, whose factory was finally closed down in 1934 when the lease was bought by the company and the buildings demolished.

We have valuable independent information concerning the working of the company during the years 1906–14 from the late Bill Riches, who joined the City warehouse in 1905 as an errand boy, and Alf Pearce, who also started at the City warehouse. Both were subsequently transferred to West Ham, where, after the war, Bill Riches became foreman in the black shop and Alf Pearce took the same position in the colour shop. In a letter to the present chairman, written in 1964, Alf Pearce remembers the West Ham factory:

Section of the black shop at West Ham 1935

General view of the black shop at West Ham 1936. At this period all machinery was
driven by belts and shafts. The vertical mill at the back was a high speed 4 roll Buhler
(Swiss) mill; at that time new to the British printing ink industry

Bill Riches senior, who worked for the company from 1905–55

A group of long service employees:
A. Gwinnell 1915–63, G. Warwick 1924–69, A. Pearce 1909–60, W. Cook 1923–64

'It consisted of two small farm sheds for the colour shop, with a smaller building along one side as a black shop and a similar place on the other side for the varnish house. . . . The colour shop had six granite roller mills on one side and four on the other, plus a bench for crushing some dry colours. . . . The power for the machinery was a small gas engine, and in the cold weather we had to help push the fly wheel round to get it started. . . . The mixing was done direct on the mill, as there were no mixers, and even a cheap poster ink (about 6d or 9d a lb) had to be mixed on the mill. . . . There were two 1 cwt scales, but no decimal scales, and for the majority of colours the recipes were so many scoops of each different colour. . . .'

According to Bill Riches, when he was first transferred to the West Ham factory in 1912, the staff there consisted of 12 employees as follows: works manager (Fred Gatward senior), varnishmaker, engineer, six colour shop employees, three black shop employees. Wages of senior employees were then about 30s per week but the company was regarded as a good employer and most employees received an increase every year, even if it was only one or two shillings.

At that time the company manufactured principally news ink litho colours and poster letterpress inks. News ink was produced by mixing Ling's black in news ink oil in large 'pugs'. These were in essence a 100 gallon container with a stirrer. After mixing in the pug (a very dirty job because the black flew all over the shop) the paste was transferred to a 30 inch mill fitted with granite rollers and finished off by another pass through a steel roller mill. Black letterpress inks were manufactured on smaller mills, sometimes in a linseed oil varnish, more often in a mixture of varnish and mineral oil. The quality of these blacks was so bad that few repeat orders were received and the only market outlet was therefore abroad.

Coloured ink was manufactured from linseed varnish and weak colour pigments, being either mineral pigments dry ground on to an extender base, or dyestuffs, usually fugitive, 'wetstruck' on an alumina-blanc-fixe base. The colour arrived in lump form and was broken down firstly, as Alf Pearce recalls, by rolling with a hand roller on a flat table. The colour was then transferred to a granite mill for 'mixing-in'; there were no mechanical mixers in the colour shop. When the 'mixing-in' process was complete, the colour was then transferred to another granite roll mill through which it passed six or eight times. It was finished off on a steel roll mill and finally potted into tins. The labour cost even in those days was significant; and even cheap poster letterpress inks, selling at 9d per lb, were made in the same way.

The recipes for coloured inks were usually discussed on the telephone between Maurice Coates and Fred Gatward senior, all the buying being done by Maurice. When the ink was finished, two samples were retained in a parchment skin and filed, together with the name of the customer and a rough recipe. There was no weighing and each repeat delivery had to be 'shaded up' to the original sample. Once a week, duplicate samples of everything made during the week were taken to George Coates's home at Buckhurst Hill and retained by him, as security for any future 'walk out'.

The varnish house at this time consisted of a shed with about five 60 gallon pots and one 20 gallon pot kept specially clean for the manufacture of bronze blue oil. This was a Coates speciality product which imparted to iron blues (Prussian Blue) a fine sheen or lustre, then in much demand from litho printers. These pots were enamelled iron inside and mild steel outside. They were heated over coal fires to make linseed oil varnish for grinding colours and rosin oil for blacks. The raw linseed oil was tanked before use for a minimum of six months and more frequently a year, in order to allow the natural sediment of 'foots' to settle out. It then was pumped out of the top of the tank by a hand pump and transferred by containers to the varnish house, for manufacture into varnish.

Little change took place in the method of manufacturing inks and varnishes (except for the introduction from Germany of improved organic pigments) until after the First World War; and it was not until the later '20s that the concept of laboratory development and control was introduced, with a view to ensuring quality control and repetitive formulation of inks by consistent recordings and accurate testing. No photographs have survived of the factory as it was before the First World War, but an artist's impression gives some idea of the factory's appearance in the '90s. The house on the left of the gate, known as Bill Warwick's cottage, was still standing in its original form at the end of the 1920s, when it was partially demolished and rebuilt as a store.

The oil boiling facilities shown on the right certainly existed in a primitive form, from the very early days. The total site area of the original factory was about half an acre and this was not enlarged until 1934, when the site of Ling's Black Factory (about 1 acre) was acquired.

During the years before and immediately after the First World War, working conditions at West Ham Factory were very bad, and the situation remained virtually unchanged until 1929. Varnish fumes choked those at work when the wind was in the wrong direction, while the fumes from Berk's Acid Works close by corroded the iron work, and contaminated tins with a film of sulphur dioxide so badly that they all had to be polished before they were fit to go out to a customer. It is something of a relief, therefore, to record that, in spite of these conditions, the factory employees mostly maintained good health and lived a normal span of life.

Despite the frequently grim conditions of work at West Ham, morale among the employees remained very high. Fred Gatward, after a prolonged absence from work in 1928 due to bronchitis, wrote thus to Maurice Coates:

'It is very painful to me to admit (through indifferent health) I am not able to

carry out my principle of the firm's progress, which I have always had at
heart, but it would be more so to think I was impeding that progress';
and later, having recovered somewhat, he wrote in the following terms in reply
to the directors' offer of early retirement and pension:

'I have no ambition for a pension while I can work. Unfortunately my health
has suffered bad luck lately, but I do not think it is (sufficiently) permanent to
call for a pension.'

Light delivery van about 1932

The picture shows Fred Parsons, the driver, with the first motor delivery van which the
company operated. This van was built on the chassis of a Willys Overland car,
originally belonging to Maurice Coates; note the solid tyres

41

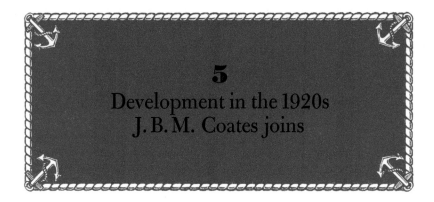

5

Development in the 1920s
J. B. M. Coates joins

After 1916, as a result of the War and the call up of young men, the company's printing ink business dwindled rapidly. Maurice joined a volunteer regiment and commanded a platoon; his regiment, which consisted mainly of medically rejected men (Maurice himself had very short sight), was scheduled to go to France in 1918 and arrangements had already been made for Mrs Maurice Coates to manage the business when fortunately the war ended before the regiment left England. From 1917 onwards large quantities of airplane dope had been manufactured at West Ham under sub-contract from Cellon Ltd, paint manufacturers to the aircraft industry. This dope was based upon nitro-cellulose and ethylacetate; it was used to impregnate and shrink the fabric stretched over the wooden framework of the wings of aircraft (which at that time were being produced at the rate of more than 1,000 planes per month). The work was so unpleasant that the operatives could only spend two to three hours at a time in the shop when this material, so essential to the war effort, was manufactured.

An important source of information concerning the operation of West Ham during this period was Frank Gatward, who joined the company in 1919 as an office boy and clerk, working under his father. Following demobilisation, which after the First World War was very rapid, there was a short lived boom when all industry was extremely busy. Bill Riches remembers there being about 18 employees in 1919–20 compared with 12 in the pre-war years. A second gas engine had been installed just before the war and the total turnover of the company at this time had risen to £60,000, equivalent to about £40,000 at pre-war prices. In 1921, however, there was a serious industrial slump and for six months the factory went on short time, so that sales turnover for the year dropped rapidly to £40,000 – a huge reduction.

Normal hours of work in those days were 8 am to 6 pm and 8 am to 1 pm on Saturdays. During the short time period the factory was closed on Saturday mornings and Mondays. When business revived in 1922, most of the factory employees joined the NATSOPA Union, with the active encouragement of the liberal minded Maurice. George, his father, appears to have been quite indifferent over what course was adopted.

Frank Gatward's description of the factory, its mills and the method of varnish making differ little from that of others who worked at West Ham. The varnishmaker at this time (1922) he remembers was a certain Starkey. He had no thermometer, no time clock and no method of determining viscosity except by pouring a little varnish into a tin lid and examining its flow characteristics. Frank Gatward recalled that the viscosity of the resulting varnish and hence its degree of polymerisation varied greatly according to the position of the varnish in the pot itself. There were no stirrers.

From 1925 onwards, Maurice made big efforts to improve the quality and consistency of varnish-making, which he recognised as an important factor in the working qualities of all inks. A new half ton kettle of stainless steel, fitted with a stirrer, was installed in 1926 and a skilled varnishmaker, Bill Speller, was recruited. This kettle was designed by the Gas Light & Coke Company and fired by gas instead of coal. Viscosity of varnish was then controlled by the test tube bubble method and the resulting quality and consistency was greatly improved.

Employees of West Ham factory during the lunch break, summer 1936

In 1926 also, a rudimentary laboratory was started with a part-time chemist, a Mr Koekoek, who had been previously employed in the paint industry and later became a technical salesman for ICI Dyestuffs. Mr Koekoek did no more than establish the laboratory in a small shed behind the office, and worked but one day a week. However, this laboratory was greatly improved when Lance (Maurice's second son) took charge of it, with Jimmy Lester (now with his own business in Canada – Lester Inks and Chemicals Ltd) as his assistant. This early laboratory was soon afterwards largely destroyed by fire and in 1930 a much improved establishment was set up in a new building.

In December 1922, Frank Gatward was transferred to the City office at St Bride's House to help with the bookkeeping, which was in a deplorable state. He remembers the office at this time as consisting of an accountant, Mr E. T. D. Garlick, himself and A. W. Cook as ledger clerks and two typists. Both Mr Garlick and Frank were fresh faces; the previous book-keeper/accountant, a Mr Varley, had been dismissed for embezzlement, and many of the customer accounts, when Frank Gatward took over the ledgers, were months behind. Mr Garlick and Frank Gatward set up a new ledger system based on very large ledgers size 50 × 30 inches weighing about 40 lb each. The original ledgers are still preserved.

The sales force consisted of the redoubtable Mr Hart, who was subsequently appointed a director, a Mr H. Garlick who retired in 1931 aged 70, Billy Watts who retired in 1930 aged 72, and a Mr Goatley who died in 1927 aged 75. This elderly sales team was increased and its average age reduced when A. W. Cook started travelling in 1922 at the age of 22, and A. C. Baker moved out of the office in 1928.

When Mr Goatley died in 1927, Maurice set about improving the quality of the sales team. Charles Butterfant, an experienced book salesman, was appointed to take over Mr Goatley's accounts; and Billy Rea, a lithographer from Belfast, was attached to the Manchester depot to take over most of the northern accounts previously in the hands of Mr Hart, who retired through ill health in 1928 at the age of 68. During the early '20s the company's share of the market gradually deteriorated; its poor manufacturing facilities and ageing sales force were no match for the much more vigorous competition deployed by firms such as Lorilleux & Bolton, under the capable leadership of H. C. Bolton, Ault and Wiborg, an American company managed from 1923 by Angus Kennedy, and B. Winstone & Sons Ltd, from 1922 managed by Eric Muirsmith, whose father was chairman and managing director of Fleming in Edinburgh who had acquired Winstones a few years previously.

The sales turnover* of the company during this period shows clearly how, in a rapidly expanding market, the company's share of the increase was much less than it was in the '30s when, under Maurice's full leadership, the company made real progress. During the later '20s Maurice's two sons, John and Lance, both of whom had been brought up with the idea of coming into the company, were gradually introduced. John worked in the colour shop during the University long vacation in 1927 and Lance spent six months working under the engineer, Chapman, from October 1928, before transferring to the laboratory. John spent

*see page 98

Annual outing ('beanfeast') July 1925. In the front row, standing from left to right:
A. Lindsay, A. Chapman, C. M. Coates, George Coates, W. Warwick

Long service employees at the company's Jubilee Year 1927. Back row: A. Lindsay, Bill
Warwick, C. M. Coates, W. Griffin, W. Riches, A. Pearce. Sitting: W. Watts, A. Hart,
Jim Barnett, Fred Gatward senior, J. Brew

a second vacation in 1928 working in the laboratory of the pigment factory of Oliver Wilkins Ltd, Derby, then part of the recently formed ICI Group.

Early in 1929 Maurice at last persuaded his father, George, to erect a much needed new building to improve the colour shop. The cost of this extension, approved in June 1929, was £1,983. Shortly afterwards George Coates, managing director since the formation of the company in 1889, died suddenly on 3 September 1929. On the day of his funeral, West Ham factory was closed and most of the employees were present at the service. Although of a shy disposition, George was well respected and especially kind to young people starting in the company. During the severe crisis of 1900 to 1902, he faced up to the difficulties with the result that the company gradually recovered. If, in later years, his restrictive financial control was overdone, at any rate the reasons for it could be understood in the past; and without a cautious financial policy the company might not have survived the various stresses which were encountered during the first 20 years of the century.

Following George's death, Maurice was appointed managing director in his place and John, his son, became a director. Colonel Hain, first appointed a director in 1905, remained as chairman until he, too, died on 12 April 1932. John Coates senior had died in 1925, so this was truly the end of an era.

A Coates Brothers cricket team about 1928

Back row left to right: 12th man, Mr Baker sen., scorer, P. Gatward, G. Coates (founder), A. Leighton, Lance Coates. Middle row, seated: Frank Gatward, C. M. Coates, J. White, W. J. Hart (director), A. C. Baker, J. B. M. Coates. Front row: L. Ludlam, C. Butterfant

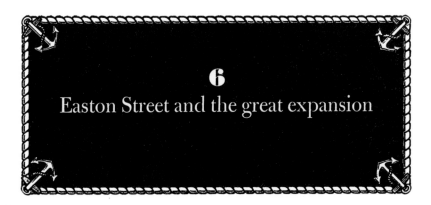

6
Easton Street and the great expansion

Now, at last, Maurice was his own master, and he quickly set about improving the manufacturing facilities at West Ham, and developing a younger sales team, so that the company might compete on equal terms with its rivals. For the latter were thick on the ground and at least half a dozen well-managed companies, in addition to the three mentioned earlier, provided keen and effective competition. From now, for a decade, the company made rapid progress, as will be apparent from the details of sales turnover shown on page 98. In the five-year period 1929–34, building works and the installation of new machinery at West Ham factory, costing £34,027, were completed; a figure which makes dramatic comparison with total fixed assets, before the programme started, of £6,679. Then in 1934, as we have seen, the lease of Ling's factory was purchased, the old buildings demolished and new buildings erected.

However, the company's growth was so rapid that even this additional space was considered to be inadequate for future needs. In 1936, therefore, the original St Mary Cray factory site, extending to 2.9 acres, was purchased for £3,000. A new factory was completed there in 1937 and the old West Ham factory, which had served the company for nearly 60 years, was evacuated and sold to F. W. Berk & Co. Ltd for £11,500.

Changes were taking place, too, in London. The St Bride's House offices had been provided with much-needed extra space by incorporating the warehouse area and taking the lease of another floor; Maurice Coates had decided some years before to establish a Printers' Sundries department in a basement underneath Salisbury Square House, a large office building in Salisbury Square. The area leased was subsequently extended to provide facilities for blending production of inks, and also of stocks for deliveries within the London area. This arrangement was never wholly satisfactory, the warehouse being situated 100 yards away from the offices, so that in 1938, new premises were purchased at Easton Street, WC1, where the company still has its headquarters. The building, put up as a speculative factory by John Laing and Son Ltd, had been originally

Easton Street, Rosebery Avenue, London WC1. Head Office of the Coates Group of Companies, first built 1938; top floor added and enlarged to incorporate the building opposite 1953 and 1960 respectively

designed with four storeys, but only three were in fact built; of these the company occupied two (the ground floor as a warehouse and southern blending factory, the first floor as a laboratory and offices) and the remaining floor was let on a long lease to Berkertex Clothes at 2s per square foot. To acquire these premises, the company negotiated a £20,000 long term mortgage; the cost of its new home was £50,000, and it is interesting to note that, when a third floor was added in 1955, this cost almost exactly the same sum.

Nor were these the only developments with which the company was concerned. Blending factories or depots were opened in Leeds (1934) and Glasgow (1936), while the first overseas companies were established in South Africa (Durban) 1936 and India (Calcutta) in 1937. On the technical side, a method of manufacturing finished inks in any quantity, except blacks, by blending concentrates, had been established by Lance Coates after visits to America and a nine-month stay in the Argentine; in the latter country, he had successfully established, in association with an English firm known as Shepherd & Co., an inkmaking operation, manufacturing ink from imported pigment dispersions (concentrates) which competed effectively with highly capitalised dry colour producers. The principles of this 'concentrate' system he picked up during a visit to the United States and it took many years for the company's competitors to adopt these same principles – without which the establishment of small scale local manufacturing units is uneconomic.

The emphasis was now on improving the company's technology, which Maurice Coates saw as being of paramount importance, and regular visits were made to the United States, and also to Germany and Austria; one example of the experience thus gained is that the flushed colour system developed in the latter countries was preferred to the large scale grinding methods of dispersion used in the United States.

Coates Brothers were the first inkmakers to join the Paint and Varnish Research Association. In 1932 a full time graduate chemist, recruited from Titanine Ltd, an industrial paint manufacturer, was appointed and in 1935 Dr Askew joined the company as chief research chemist, Lance Coates remaining as technical director until the West Ham factory was closed.

It was during this period that the company secured its first technical breakthrough with the successful formulation, firstly of Neoset blacks, and subsequently (and more fundamentally) of Neoset process colours. The Neoset principle of a two phase drying system was invented in 1935. In the case of blacks, the process was a successful competitor of but never a substitute for the earlier Superset inks introduced by Dr Bowles of Lorilleux & Bolton and based upon blown castor oil. When applied to process colour inks, the Neoset principle unexpectedly provided an almost perfect solution to the problem of 'refusal'. Before the introduction of these inks, process printing was a difficult art, involving considerable risk when overprinting one colour upon another,

49

success depending upon the amount of drier incorporated in the ink and the time interval between different printings. With Neoset inks these difficulties were largely eliminated, and almost overnight the company was able to penetrate in large volume the lucrative and growing market for process colour inks. Great efforts were made by the company's competitors to match these inks, entirely without success during the pre-war period. Tony Harrison (the company's production director until December 1976) can recall the desperate efforts made by Winstones to find the secret of these simple recipes. In today's circumstances, it seems strange that these secrets were never leaked and that the lead enjoyed by these inks remained until equivalent competitive products were gradually developed in the early 1950s.

Early tanker delivering Chinese Tung oil. This was a drying oil then used extensively for the manufacture of overprint varnish and Gold ink, The price in 1932 was £45 per ton (1977, £1,800)

The company's technology in manufacturing improved offset inks was less successful, but from 1934 onwards strenuous efforts were made to manufacture gravure inks, then successfully made only by one or two competitors. For this purpose, a German chemist was employed, but his recipes proved to be of little use. More successful was the gradual improvement in technology developed with the help of several friendly printers, of whom Hector Hough, who later joined the company as a branch manager in Liverpool, was one of the early pioneers.

During the five years which led up to the Second World War, the company was finally successful in acquiring a major share of the fast growing market for gravure inks (other than for periodicals); this was due almost entirely to the technological excellence of its products. The development of these products was greatly helped by John Hand's experience with cellulose and other industrial paints based on solvents, when at Titanine; but an important additional reason for success was the decision to develop specialist technical personnel, a policy which led immediately after the war to the establishment of entirely separate liquid ink laboratories under the control of Fred Hough, nephew of Hector. These laboratories and the separate manufacturing facilities at St Mary Cray factory laid the foundation of the company's lead in liquid ink technology: and this in turn has been a prominent feature of the post-war pattern of sales development in all territories where the company has established factories.

Just before the war in 1939, Coates secured another technical break-through when heatset inks working at a web speed of 250 ft per minute were successfully demonstrated to David Greenhill, managing director of Sun Engraving Co. Ltd. At this time, Mr Greenhill was probably the most highly regarded printing technician in England. He immediately saw the value of the demonstration, the inks for which were an adaptation of the Neoset principle, and forthwith ordered, against the wishes of his own staff, one of his Hoe-Crabtree presses to be equipped with the necessary heaters. The progress of these developments was interrupted by the war, but immediately after the war Rotary Printing Heaters Ltd was registered as a subsidiary company to convert existing rotary presses to print heatset. A significant measure of success was achieved but with the introduction of more sophisticated heaters as an integral part of new rotary presses, it soon became apparent that the engineering technology involved was outside the scope of the company's experience; so that Rotary Printing Heaters Ltd was gradually phased out of existence. This was, perhaps, one reason why in the late '50s, Coates, although first in the heatset field, lost an important technical lead which was not regained until the '70s.

Pictorial letterhead in use by the company 1938–48

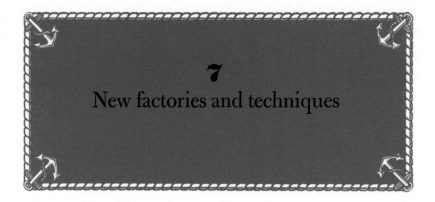

7
New factories and techniques

In 1946 a major decision was taken, which had far reaching results, leading among other things, to the acquisition of another factory: this was to embark upon the serious manufacture of synthetic resins. John Coates had persuaded his father, rather against the latter's will, that the manufacture of synthetic resins as the principal film former for printing inks was technically more important than the manufacture of pigment colours, which were traditionally produced by large printing ink manufacturers. One of the principal reasons for the manufacture of synthetic resins was that all advanced printing ink manufacturers had great difficulty in purchasing resins suitable for the manufacture of printing inks rather than paints.

The company had been manufacturing such resins on a small scale since 1938 and a selling company, Cray Valley Products Ltd, had been registered the same year. Moreover, its experience during the war of making surface coating synthetic resins and oleo-resinous synthetic vehicles as sub-contractors for various wartime specifications, only reinforced John's determination to embark upon the manufacture of these materials. It was soon clear, however, that such manufacture on any sufficient scale would be impossible at St Mary Cray; and thus another basic factory site was sought and a public issue of preference capital later promoted to finance the construction of a new factory. These plans eventually bore fruit in the selection of the South Wales factory site at Machen and its development during the last 25 years as the largest single manufacturing unit in the Coates Group of Companies.

At the beginning of the venture, John's ideas were treated with scepticism by his father and viewed with misgivings by some of his senior colleagues. But the project proceeded and the first large reactor at the South Wales factory was commissioned in November 1951: and so successful has the progress of this factory been ever since, that today it incorporates not only one of the largest synthetic resin production units in Europe, but also units specialising in the manufacture of metal coatings products and multi-metal lithographic plates, which were added subsequently.

Road tankers at South Wales factory loading synthetic resin for delivery to
customers of Cray Valley Products Ltd

Factory employees at St Mary Cray c.1950

This enterprise led to a change in the status of the company. In order to get it started and to raise the necessary finance, the company became a public company and in January 1948, £200,000 of $4\frac{1}{2}$% redeemable preference capital was raised through a public issue. The ordinary shares were not at first listed, but subsequently a stock exchange quotation was obtained, through an introduction in June 1949.

The development of the South Wales factory site (45 acres) has proceeded without interruption and has proved to be a magnificent base on which to build the supremacy of the Resin Division and the Finishes Division. The early stages of site preparation (1948–51) and factory development (1951–54) necessitated learning many lessons. The problems of site preparation within the cost limits imposed by the company's limited resources were effectively tackled by an extremely capable Czech engineer and surveyor, who came to the company by chance as a refugee labourer following his expulsion from Czechoslovakia as

Aerial view of South Wales factory 1975. At this date approximately 18 acres of the 45-acre site had been developed

54

a result of the communist take-over. The first building was erected in 1952. It consisted of a large aircraft hangar (16,000 sq. ft purchased for £4,000) adapted for storage purposes, and with the first Wales offices and laboratories built inside the main fabric; a specialist building to house the first resin reactor; a filter press annexe and a separate boiler house completed the initial factory buildings. Finally the first 5-ton resin reactor was installed and commissioned for production in August 1953. The problems of plant design and factory layout for resin manufacturing purposes were greatly helped by visits to United States factories made in the main by Andrew Ruck (appointed technical director of the company in 1954). One of these visits led to the negotiation of the initial licensing arrangement for the manufacture of polyamide resins from the General Mills Corporation, thereby initiating an association which has been mutually rewarding and beneficial to both companies, and which still continues.

Two other basic factories were acquired and developed during the post-war

Aerial view of Midsomer Norton factory 1976 showing 11-acre site formerly a coal mine

Aerial view of Johnson Riddle factory acquired 1976 and renamed
St Mary Cray South

Aerial view of St Mary Cray factory 1976 occupying the whole of a 5-acre site

period. Thirteen acres of land on the site of an old coal mine at Midsomer Norton, Somerset, were purchased in 1968 and have now been developed as a basic factory for the manufacture of liquid inks for the printing ink division and as the headquarters and principal factory of the reprographic division. On this site was also established an important blending factory for the supply of finished products to Bristol and the west of England.

Even more recently, in 1970, an opportunity occurred to purchase the ailing synthetic resin business of Laporte-Synres, situated on five acres of land at Stallingborough in the Humber estuary (this factory was originally established as a branch of a Dutch company). The site area has subsequently been extended to eight acres and the manufacturing facilities greatly improved by the installation of additional large reactors and blenders. During the same period, the St Mary Cray factory was extended and developed, and the recent acquisition of another nearby factory has made available an additional 45,000 sq. ft of floor area. Throughout the UK, the regional factories of the printing ink division have been enlarged and rebuilt, and in the Republic of Ireland an excellent site for the development of another basic factory was acquired with the purchase of the Glenside Printing Ink Co. Ltd during 1956.

New synthetic resin reactor, Stallingborough factory 1976, used in the manufacture of polyester and specialist alkyd resins

8
The start of overseas operations

The idea of establishing what he called 'Service Stations' (by which he meant blending factories) in the British Empire territories had always appealed to Maurice Coates. India was then the largest export market for British printing ink manufacturers, and during the early '30s discussions were accordingly initiated with a wealthy Indian who was interested in financing Maurice's idea. Despite his father's enthusiasm, John was always sceptical at this stage, believing that the company did not yet have the resources to embark upon enterprises of this nature; but with the rapid growth of the company in the home market and its much stronger financial position, Maurice was determined to start at least one overseas company.

Accordingly, in 1935 he visited South Africa to discuss this with his brother George; and together they agreed to establish a new company in Durban – the first South African printing ink manufacturer. Coates Brothers (South Africa) Pty Ltd was opened in 1936 with Denys Heesom as its managing director and Allen Goodwin, a 20-year-old technician from the Manchester depot, as technical manager. The company made slow progress in its early years but with the outbreak of war in Europe in 1939, imports were so badly interrupted that the new company had a golden opportunity – which it seized – to become the principal supplier of printing ink products throughout the then Union of South Africa.

Two years later, Maurice travelled again to South Africa and also visited India; this trip resulted in the establishment of a small blending unit in Calcutta, in association with the Indian branch of the company's advertising agents, D. J. Keymer & Co. Ltd. This production unit was opened as a branch of the London company towards the end of 1937, under the management of Percy Gatward. With his friendly personality and technical skill, Percy Gatward soon established a regular trade and became a veritable printing ink 'doctor'. By the start of the war, the business was able to sell all it could produce, and thereafter it became a major supplier of inks to the Indian Ordnance Survey, for the printing of wartime maps for the East Asian campaigns.

South African Directors and Secretary 1959
Left to right: A. E. Goodwin, F. H. Y. Bamford, G. W. Coates, Chairman,
T. Harris-Matthews, Secretary, H. D. A. Heesom, Managing Director

Entire Works staff of Durban factory, 29 Turner's Avenue, 1938
Left to right, back row: John Turner, printing ink technician, Mani Ramgoolam,
millman, Lall Ramgoolam, millman, Ram Ramgoolam, packer. Front row: Ben and
Tom (second names unknown)

Percy Gatward 1922–56, who started the Indian business in 1937 and was a Director of Coates of India Limited 1947–56

A. O. Ellison, first Chairman of Coates Brothers Australia Pty Ltd 1950–74

In 1947 the Indian business was reconstituted as a rupee company and progressed rapidly until it became the leading printing ink manufacturer on the Indian sub-continent. John Coates visited South Africa for the first time in 1948 and India in 1952 to learn at first hand the problems of developing these companies in an unfamiliar environment.

But these ventures were still a small part of Maurice Coates's vision. He pressed continuously for the establishment of comparable businesses in Australia and New Zealand against the judgment of John who saw the difficulties due to lack of skilled staff and the existence of already well established indigenous manufacturers in both territories. Nothing daunted, however, Maurice made a long trip to Australia and New Zealand in 1949, returning full of enthusiasm to begin manufacturing operations. But his plans were still resisted by John (who knew that he would be responsible for the success or failure of these companies) and who considered that the difficulties of forming such companies now were too great.

So matters might have remained, if it had not been for the inability of Australian manufacturers to produce acceptable periodical gravure inks. During his visit, Maurice was approached concerning this problem and, as a result, several large shipments of gravure inks were imported. The quality of these inks proved vastly superior to the local product with the result that an approach was made from the largest non captive user to establish a factory. In these circumstances John's opposition weakened and he made his first visit to

60

Australia and New Zealand in 1952. Even so, this project might never have developed further had it not been for the negotiating skill of Mr A. O. Ellison, a Sydney lawyer who became chairman of the local company, in somewhat unusual circumstances.

Mr Ellison, who was chairman of Coates Brothers Australia Pty Ltd from its foundation in 1950 until he retired in 1974, joined the company as a result of a discussion which took place a few hours before Maurice was due to leave Sydney for England in his ship. He called, unexpectedly, at Mr Ellison's office in O'Connell Street and was received by Miss Elliott, his secretary and assistant. Maurice was informed that Mr Ellison never saw people except by appointment, but this did not deter him. Maurice was very tall and Miss Elliott was short; she could not get rid of him as he paced around the office saying he would wait, so she went back to her boss and asked what she should do. At Miss Elliott's request and description of the intruder, Mr Ellison agreed to see Maurice 'but for five minutes only'; this was a strict condition, so he was ushered into the presence. Maurice Coates could exercise great charm when he wished, but so could Owen Ellison. For two minutes they both fenced with each other and then Maurice saw some pictures of racehorses on the walls. He walked up to one and asked Mr Ellison if he were a breeder. This, of course, was a very shrewd enquiry, although a trifle lucky, because it so happened that Owen Ellison was one of the leading breeders in Australia. The conversation then switched to blood lines, genetic inheritance, the objectives of breeding and its hazards. All this took almost an hour. Finally, Maurice took the initiative and said he must go but he also said that he knew that Mr Ellison would now consent to be chairman of Coates Australia. He assured him that no real work would be involved – 'my son will see to all that'. Thus it was that it was left to the son and Owen Ellison himself to forge a close relationship which, over many years, enabled the company to survive through a series of vicissitudes which would have killed most companies.

John refused to build a liquid inks factory without a long term contract, as there was only one major customer; he wanted a ten year contract but it was unheard of for any Australian to sign any such document. However, during long negotiations extending over many weeks, the contract was eventually secured and arrangements to build and operate a factory at Auburn NSW, under the management of John Craig, were completed. The factory opened in 1953, since when the development of the Australian company as one of the major producers in that territory has been continuous. Nevertheless, John's reservations proved correct and the difficulties of creating a profitable company in the Australian environment have proved greater than anywhere else.

Meantime, the company had been approached by a local New Zealand import agency – Neill Cropper & Co. Ltd, with a request to help them manage a small printing ink company which they had acquired. This was Lorilleux & Bolton

J. R. Cropper, Chairman of Coates Brothers (New Zealand) Ltd 1952–75

(New Zealand) Ltd, an ailing company with a turnover of only £2,000 per annum. John Coates refused to advise on the management of the company without a substantial equity holding which was eventually conceded at 33%. However, the company did not prosper in spite of the provision of an English technical manager, so that the original New Zealand owners offered to sell their shareholding. Coates Brothers (New Zealand) Ltd was then formed with the London company as 100% owner of the new company, under the leadership of Jim Cropper as chairman. In 1956 Roger Manuel was appointed general manager of the company and subsequently managing director. From that time progress was rapid and the company soon became and still remains the leading manufacturer in that territory.

Entrance to Victoria factory of Coates Brothers Australia Pty Ltd, at Moorabbin, Melbourne, completed for occupation 1961

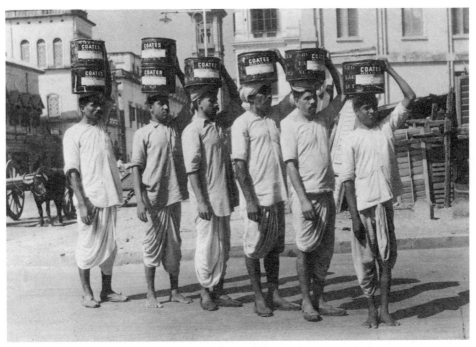

Delivering ink by coolie from Calcutta factory November 1939. This was the standard way of delivering ink in those days

Front view of Coates Brothers Australia Pty Ltd, Auburn factory, Sydney

9
Overseas expansion gets underway

Following the establishment of Coates in Australia and New Zealand, additional overseas companies were started in Rhodesia (1954), Singapore (1958), Kenya (1959), Malaysia (1963), Hong Kong (1965), Zambia (1966), Trinidad (1967), Jamaica (1969) and West Africa (1973). The formation of these companies involved a great deal of planning, both in London and on the spot overseas, and for almost 20 years, John visited each overseas company every other year, travelling to Asia and Australasia one winter and to Africa (and very often the United States too) the following winter. In every case, staff had to be trained in England, factories had to be built and local selling and commercial organisations developed. In this exacting task John was greatly helped by the personnel in the Overseas Department and visits made to the various countries by senior management; notable among such travellers was Mr Harrison, who in association with local architects built and commissioned no less than 6 basic and 15 subsidiary factories during the period 1955 to 1975.

John found these visits very arduous, and increasingly so as the years passed; but they were enjoyable too and enabled him to visit many interesting areas of the world. Although constantly pressed for time on his travels, he managed to keep a diary recording his impression of the many interesting places he visited and the difficult circumstances in which he was often placed: such problems included riots in India, accommodation difficulties on early visits to Australia and New Zealand and, after independence in the African territories, the ever present danger of unpleasant police action if, by any chance, an accident in the car took place. Those accustomed to today's aircraft have little appreciation of the hazards, delays and fatigue suffered by long distance air travellers in the '50s before the introduction of jet engines. Not only were the propeller planes much slower but they were notoriously unreliable and it was rare to make a long distance journey without at least one lengthy interruption for repairs. Despite the discomforts, however, John and those who accompanied him – including especially Peter Piercy with his unusual facility for exuding a nostalgia for

The entire staff of Johannesburg factory 1962

New basic factory at Isipingo, near Durban, South Africa, completed 1969

Basic factory of Coates of India Ltd at Chandivli, Bombay, completed 1963

First basic factory and present Head Office of Coates Brothers (South Africa) Ltd,
Cape Town

suburbia in the most exotic surroundings – were all aware that they were participating in a great adventure, and did their best to make it a successful one. This applied more particularly to those who followed him, whether as expatriates or emigrants, who set out to establish manufacturing companies in unfamiliar territories. The early Coates overseas companies did, in fact, become very successful in the '60s, and it was assumed by many that this was due solely to the company's technological lead. In fact, nearly all the companies had difficulties at the beginning, and John's view that a company is only as good as its skilled staff and, especially, its chief executive, has subsequently proved only too true.

In 1968 the directors took a conscious decision to move into Europe without, however, appreciating fully the additional difficulties of establishing any manufacturing project in Europe, due to the language problem and the very different cultural background. For many years, considerable success had been achieved by two associate companies – Drubin in Denmark, and Prisma in Spain, who were advised both managerially and technically by the company's experts. In neither case, however, was the company responsible for staff selection or management.

Thus it was that in 1968 the Vendelboe Company was purchased in Norway and in 1969 a small company was purchased in France and subsequently reconstituted as a Coates company based on a new factory at Pontoise. In both cases, considerable difficulties were encountered following the retirement of the former managements and these difficulties have persisted until recently, when an entirely new approach to European development has opened up good prospects of putting these companies on a secure foundation.

Similar improvements in the performance and prospects of the European companies managed by the Synthetic Resin and Reprographic divisions is now apparent. Overall, therefore, the situation is encouraging for the future.

New factory of Coates Brothers (Singapore) Pte Ltd, completed 1975

10
Overseas organisation 1947–77
by J. B. M. Coates
Managing Director 1948–70, Chairman 1956–77

In 1947 the sales turnover of the only two overseas companies then established – South Africa and India – was £215,000 which, aggregated with the sales of the parent company, gave a total for the year 31 October 1947 of £1,221,000. In 1976, the sales turnover of 14 overseas companies, excluding 5 European companies, totalled £30.36 million out of a consolidated group turnover of £75 million; thus within 30 years the money value of sales turnover of the overseas organisation increased by 141 times or, if discounted for inflation, by not less than 28 times. This rapid growth was achieved by internal development and financed by retained earnings of the parent and local subsidiary companies. During the same period the nett assets of all companies in the group increased from £0.663 million in 1948 to £32.94 million in 1976.

How was this transformation achieved without any significant external acquisitions? Part of the answer lies in the fact that the company was able to provide in the territories selected a facility which was almost non-existent: the provision through local manufacture of printing inks and, subsequently, other graphic supplies and metal coatings for consumption by the local printing industries.

From the early colonial days the printing industry was one of the first important industries to be established locally, because of its requirement for close personal contact with its customers. Sizeable printing industries existed in all the British Empire territories in 1939 and, except for Australia, almost all supplies for these industries were imported. Imported printing ink could not be made to suit special local circumstances and, if unsuitable, could never be returned.

When, therefore, a local source of printing ink was established, it created immediate interest. Unfortunately, however, early attempts to establish indigenous ink manufacturing facilities often failed for lack of any competent inkmaker or technician. Realising this, Coates put a high priority on the provision of an experienced technician when a decision to establish a local company was taken.

A second unique feature of the early Coates companies was their ability to manufacture from standardised imported intermediates in local blending factories. The cost of establishing these factories to manufacture, initially, paste inks (letterpress and offset) was small, so that even a modest factory could become financially viable once customers' confidence in the ability of the local technician was established; for this meant that the company could then recover its increased costs by charging higher prices for its products than the prices at which competitive imports were available. This simple principle of manufacturing paste inks in small blending factories established in the principal markets was subsequently extended, with modifications, to the manufacture of liquid inks (gravure and flexo) and metal coatings products. As the business grew, more basic manufacturing methods were introduced, with the end result that the production technology employed in the largest companies was comparable with the advanced techniques used by the parent company. The largest overseas company – South Africa – now manufactures a complete range of printing ink products entirely from basic materials; it is also a major supplier of graphic supplies, of which litho chemicals and printers' rollers are manufactured locally. In recent years, too, new divisions have been established making synthetic resins and reprographic materials for the copying industry.

The South African company in 1977 employed about 480 people. Its development has been typical of companies within the group, and a brief description of the philosophy behind its growth and the methods used to promote it may provide an insight into the development of the whole overseas organisation.

I made my first visit to South Africa in 1948. I decided from the outset that I should remain in the country long enough to understand the problems of the local company in relation to its market; and to reach agreement with the local directors on a forward plan, extending over two to four years, for the development of technical and executive staff and the planning and financing of capital expenditure projects. After my first visit (which was longer) this plan normally involved spending four weeks in the country. As the company grew and the work load increased it still proved possible to contain future visits to four weeks, as my own knowledge increased and less time was necessary to assemble the facts to give advice upon the different problems which arose. In these later visits also I was accompanied by my personal secretary and an executive assistant from the overseas department in London.

In 1948, South Africa was a largely under-developed country as far as industry was concerned. The principal centres were widely separated and transport by air was only just beginning. Railways were slow and very hot. The South African railway gauge is 3'6" and average speeds over 30 m.p.h. were, and still are, exceptional. This narrow gauge was adopted by the early railway builders because of the steep curves necessitated by the rugged terrain and widespread rock outcrops.

But that same year (1948) the South African economy 'took off'; for almost 30 years industrial expansion continued without any serious setback. Our company has grown in step with this development so that today the company operates two basic factories and three additional blending factories.

From the beginning we set out to grow with the market. Our greatest problem was how to provide a sufficient number of qualified technical and executive personnel. From the earliest days it proved difficult to attract well-educated indigenous young people who, generally speaking, were unwilling to spend four years or so working as a trainee for a private company in a small industry when so many other opportunities in the professions, in the mining industry, or in long-established multi-national companies beckoned. Similar difficulties in recruiting high-quality young people were subsequently encountered in Australia and New Zealand.

The only solution, therefore, was to bring out people from Great Britain or Ireland, and this I started to organise on a considerable scale and with a surprising measure of success. My experience amply confirms that the spirit of enterprise and adventure is still very strong in the young people of Britain, if given the opportunity.

In other areas, expert advice from Britain, in association with local professional help, was all-important. Nowhere was this more necessary than in factory building and finance. Local architects in the southern hemisphere territories are professionally competent but, because of the high fire risk in all our factories and for other reasons, including pollution, specialised knowledge concerning design is essential. Even today this is still provided largely by the parent company and involves instructing local architects at long distance, which is never easy. As the company grew, an effective management accounting and data processing organisation assumed real importance; but as the South African economy grew too, in just the same way as happened in other economies, the supply of indigenous accountants always lagged behind, so that expatriate support in this area too has been essential.

During the most active period of the development of our overseas companies, between 1952 and 1970, it was my practice to visit the African companies (eight factories) one winter and the Asian and Australasian companies (fifteen factories) the following one. The African trip occupied about eight weeks including the outward journey by sea of 11 days; the Asian and Australasian trip occupied about three months, travelling everywhere by air, with an additional two weeks or so if visits within the USA were included. These American visits were and still are important, in view of the liaison and licensee arrangements which we have developed on a reciprocal basis.

I have often been asked how any chief executive of an important English company could afford to spend so long a time each year away from base. My answer has been two-fold: firstly, if management responsibility is properly decentralised, executive authority is not impaired; and, secondly, that with suitable assistance it is possible to keep in touch with developing matters of sufficient importance.

A more serious problem was my own stamina, or rather lack of it. Travelling extensively by air and constantly moving about is much more tiring than most men will admit; after a while this catches up with the constitution. In each territory I visited, a period of familiarisation by intensive discussions at all levels and with selected customers in the market was followed by a series of formal meetings for consultation. These meetings established the detailed pattern for the company's development over the next two years and sometimes longer.

To combat fatigue I introduced specific rest periods in all my later trips, including at least one long weekend in each country. In South Africa I would stay with my sister either on the fruit farm at Banhoek, near Stellenbosch, or at her house at Hermanus on the coast, with its miles and miles of unspoilt, sandy beaches where one can enjoy complete solitude. In Australia I was always privileged to spend one weekend at Baramul, the beautiful stud property owned by our then Chairman, Owen Ellison. I used to walk and spend many hours listening to Mr Ellison explaining and demonstrating the difficult art of breeding racehorses and showing his own great affection for their progeny.

Baramul is a large business in its own right and it is a great tribute to Mr Ellison's versatility that he has been able to develop and control this property so successfully while continuing, over many years, to conduct his local Sydney practice and act as Chairman of several important companies including our own. Baramul lies 250 miles north-west of Sydney and is reputedly the valley around which Ralph Boldre wrote that Australian classic *Robbery Under Arms*. The book describes how in the 1860s a brilliant gang of cattle rustlers used to hide stolen stock in this valley and then drive the animals, through a secret exit, overland to markets in Victoria and South Australia where their origin would be unknown.

In New Zealand I always liked to try and stay one weekend at Mount Cook, a government hotel resort in the mountains 250 miles west of Christchurch; but in New Zealand I was unlucky in that several times I became ill, once seriously. Possibly this was because New Zealand was the end of the line; as too was India when travelling the other way.

I made many friends and received many kindnesses on these long trips. In India for example, in 1965, when I was lunching in Madras with one of our major customers, it came out that I had nowhere very exciting to spend Christmas: he immediately made available his own house in the highlands of Madras at Kodai Kanal, or 'Kody' as it was affectionately known to successive generations of British people who originally established this attractive hill station. With its village green, English church and lake, Kody still resembles an English village of the late 19th century.

I found India a fascinating country, particularly outside the main cities, where the rural areas in the hill country are very attractive to visitors from England. My first visit to India in 1952 coincided with the transitional period immediately following independence, when many of the trappings of the imperial system continued unchanged. The British Army had departed but the great British industrial and commercial houses were still managed for the most part by British expatriates, although in some cases they had been sold off to Indian interests. At that time and for many years thereafter, British citizens, as members of the Commonwealth, could settle and work in India as of right; this same privilege was extended to Indian citizens who wished to reside in the United Kingdom.

As a result, for more than a decade after independence, the number of British expatriates employed in industry and commerce in the main Indian cities considerably exceeded the numbers similarly employed in the last days of the imperial system. Accordingly there continued in these cities, and especially in Calcutta, a large British community with its own social life based upon the clubs which the British people have always established for their own enjoyment and cohesion in all territories of the former British Empire. The character and extent of this social life and its degree of integration with the Indian community varied. In Bombay, for example, the 'expatriate way of life' was severely circumscribed by a form of prohibition forbidding the sale of alcoholic liquor, except for consumption in private houses by registered 'addicts'; and although it was not difficult for an expatriate resident or even a visitor to secure registration, the regulations concerning consumption did have important side effects. I saw on my last visit to India in 1969 (and it is even more so the case today) that all this has changed. Even in Calcutta, which was for more than 200 years the centre of British commercial influence in India, only a handful of expatriates now remains; and with the completion of British industrial disinvestment when all foreign companies must pass into Indian control, even these will disappear. In the case of our own company, Coates of India Ltd, the last expatriate Managing Director left in April 1977. Nevertheless, the desire to maintain contact with the British parent company remains strongly embedded in the minds of Indians; and in my opinion the problems for the future in maintaining such contacts will be financial and economic rather than political.

Building the overseas companies of the Coates organisation has been a fascinating experience, if somewhat arduous. To maintain the momentum of these companies in the face of much stronger competition and in markets which are not now expanding anything like so quickly as previously, now requires techniques and management policies different from those which I developed. Visiting directors and executives must be experienced professionals in their own right; and their visits must be regular if our technology and marketing expertise is to compete successfully against the stronger challenge of American companies in these formerly exclusive British territories. In the larger companies a different kind of local management must be developed as these businesses continue to expand and thus to demand a more sophisticated organisation and higher quality of business talent as well as technical knowledge and commercial acumen.

But although the difficulties are greater than they were, the resources of the group organisation are also much stronger. These resources need sensitive handling, however; so that one of the greatest problems in the future may well be how to keep them sufficiently flexible so that the needs of individual companies within each territory are taken fully into account.

The first factory of Coates Brothers (NZ) Ltd. which was started in a disused public house in Auckland in November 1949

The Auckland factory as it is today following the construction of a second floor office block in 1967

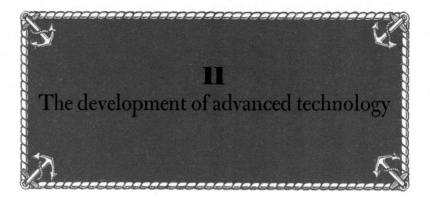

11

The development of advanced technology

Before 1939 the varnishes and grinding vehicles used by the printing ink and paint industries were still largely based on natural drying oils and fossil gums. The rapid post-war development of synthetic resin technology, in its application to the printing ink, paint, chemical coatings and adhesive industries, has amply fulfilled John Coates's original belief, that these materials would allow the formulation of greatly improved end products. In fact, it is no exaggeration to say that the nature, durability and appearance of a wide range of consumer products has been revolutionised by the increasing availability of specialist synthetic resins.

As at June 1977, 63 qualified chemists and technologists were employed in the resin division's laboratories, engaged on research and development (R and D) activities, designed to improve the long-term performance of all the company's products. R and D laboratories and separate application laboratories are located at all three of the resin division's sites at St Mary Cray, South Wales and Stallingborough. In addition, each manufacturing division maintains its own R and D laboratories – printing ink laboratories are located at St Mary Cray, finishes division laboratories at Easton Street in central London, and the laboratories of the reprographics division are at Midsomer Norton, adjacent to this division's principal factory. The plates division maintains its R and D laboratories at South Wales also adjacent to this division's production unit. Each laboratory is under the control of a senior chemist, and within the printing ink division the R and D effort is further sub-divided under main product groups.

Each divisional laboratory works in close association with the resin R and D laboratories, and all laboratories are equipped with the latest analytical instruments and machinery for testing the finished products. In the printing ink division this includes commercial printing machines, while the finishes division is equipped with a wide assortment of fabricating tools, as actually used in the rigid container industry. The reprographics division has what is probably the most comprehensive selection of copying machines assembled anywhere within the United Kingdom.

The impact of research ideas is international, and close contact is maintained at the highest technical level with research workers in industrial companies in the United States, Japan and Europe. This liaison has led to the negotiation of a number of important licensing agreements, based either on patented information or specialised knowhow. Such agreements are becoming increasingly two-way, as the value of the company's own technology achieves wider recognition in the advanced industrial countries.

Coates Brothers, therefore, through its subsidiary companies and operating divisions, is now in the very forefront of surface coatings technology as it continues to develop and cater for the ever more sophisticated needs of application. The scope of such application covers a wide range of uses from printing to decorative display and from protective coatings to electronic circuits. The company's products are regularly used either directly or as components in the manufacture of a very wide range of packaging materials and consumer durables; more recently the electronics industry is creating new demands for sophisticated products for such purposes as accelerated curing of thin film systems and instantaneous facsimile reproduction.

In summary, therefore, our technical objectives embrace every new development of polymer chemistry concerned with thin film application. This involves us ever more closely with the consumer goods revolution and the design of systems to promote the art of 'convenience living'. Thus it will be apparent, that the scope for further development of our products is still considerable.

In all our technical laboratories, therefore, we work to keep the lead we have earned.

SOME NOTED TECHNOLOGICAL ACHIEVEMENTS

One of the most important factors in promoting the rapid growth of the Coates Group of Companies has been the development of leader products, technologically superior to competitive products available at the time of their introduction. The design of these products was greatly helped by the decision to manufacture synthetic resins, the most important film former for both pigmented and unpigmented systems in the printing ink, paint and reprographic industries. It is interesting to recall, therefore, some of the more important products which have been developed over the last 40 years. A few of these are described below:

Neoset process inks

Neoset process letterpress inks were introduced on the home market in 1935; they were the first two-phase setting inks. Success was immediate, because these were the first sheet-fed inks to be touch dry almost immediately after printing. The two-phase principle enabled the oxidisation principle to take its normal course so that the inks were hard dry within about eight hours. Neoset 4-colour half-tone process inks revolutionised colour printing in those days. The two-phase principle enabled the inks to remain 'open' so that over-printing could take place within very wide time intervals and without the necessity of drier additions by the pressman. The problems of crystallisation and 'refusal' were eliminated and the success of these inks at the time when the market for process colour printing was expanding fast was immediate.

Cosol display colours

Cosol inks were the first true film screen inks for paper and board. As such they had many advantages, both in printability and appearance, over the earlier film inks which gave a much coarser print.

Unicat inks for polythene containers

Unicat inks were the first single-pack screen inks successfully applied to the printing of plastic bottles. With their durability and high finish, they are still the market leader for this type of container in many territories.

Heat transfer inks

In the early 1970s Coates Brothers Inks Limited pioneered the introduction of heat transfer inks for textile printing by gravure (Transtex) and flexo (Aquatex). The resulting transfer technique has revolutionised the printing of textiles in many territories. More recently the introduction of Fastran wet transfer inks has enabled the transfer printing process to be applied to wool, nylon and acrylic fabrics.

Leo heatset inks

Leo heatset inks were the first really successful low emission, low energy, heatset inks introduced in 1975 to overcome problems of pollution. The inks were immediately accepted and subsequently imitated by competitive products.

Offset inks

The continuous improvement of offset lithographic inks over many years has been a feature of the Coates laboratory development. The current range of Titan inks, suitable for commercial printing, and Trojan inks, especially designed for carton printing, are both leaders in their field (1977).

FINISHES DIVISION

The Finishes Division was established in 1966 as a separate company to take over the metal coatings product group, consisting of tin printing inks, coatings and lacquers, which the company had manufactured since 1946 for supply to the rigid container industry. An entirely different product group manufacturing industrial coatings for various applications was incorporated in this division at the same time. A high degree of success has been achieved through the development of leader products based upon advanced technology, amongst which the following may be mentioned:

Tube enamels
Alkyd, vinyl alkyd, epi ester and vinyl tube enamels were leaders in this difficult area of technology for many years, being resistant to almost all materials packed in tubes, and at the same time providing an attractive appearance.

Closure coatings
The company were the first manufacturers in Europe of coatings for the 'twist off' systems, previously developed in the United States. Subsequently these products were upgraded as acrylic coatings and more recently complete closure systems have been introduced to the specialist producers of these products.

Internal lacquers
Preservex (MU) lacquer was first introduced in the mid 1950s as a universal lacquer for meat and other packs. Subsequently, improved epiphenolic lacquers and aluminised meat release lacquers were adopted by the leading international manufacturers as universal materials for internal protection. In 1960 pre-solder side stripe lacquer was introduced and became the preferred product in many territories for protecting the side seam of three-piece cans.

Two-piece cans
In the mid 1970s the technique of manufacturing rigid containers by drawing and wall ironing techniques, necessitating only an easy open end to complete the can, was introduced. The internal coatings and non-varnish decorative systems for this new type of container were pioneered by the Finishes Division.

INDUSTRIAL PRODUCTS GROUP

Leading materials manufactured by this product group include mould release agents for the steel industry, sold under the trade name Alugrip; lacquers for the paper and board industry sold under the trade names of Unicol and Vioglaze, and a solventless adhesive for flexible packaging sold under the trade name Cobond.

Polyamides

Cray Valley Products Ltd were the first manufacturers of polyamide resins in Europe. These new resins, which were the product of a Ministry of Agriculture patent during the war, have made a significant contribution to polymer chemistry generally and the surface coatings industries in particular. Used principally as crosslinking agents for epoxy resins, they yield tough resistant paints which are used in the chemical, marine and aerospace industries. They also form the base of high-performance adhesives, potting compositions for the electronics industry and printing inks, more particularly inks for printing on films for packaging. Manufacture of dimer acid, the most important raw material component of these resins, was commenced in 1967 as a further extension of our technological agreements with the General Mills Corporation in America. Polyamides are sold under the trade names Versamid, Versalon, Genamid and Synolide.

Thixotropic alkyds

We were the first manufacturer of thixotropic alkyds outside the United States. Thixotropy is an important characteristic of 'structured' paints, which was subsequently adapted for the manufacture of so-called non-drip paints, the technology of which was pioneered throughout Europe by Cray Valley Products Ltd. Thixotropic alkyds are sold under the trade name Gelkyd.

Water soluble stoving resins

Water soluble resins under the trade name Resydrol were introduced as resins for the manufacture of stoving industrial finishes in the early 1960s. They were subsequently successfully adapted for use in coatings applied by electrodeposition, a process now widely adapted for priming car bodies. These resins, being free from noxious solvents, make an important contribution in areas where a pollution free environment is essential.

Cold curing acrylic resins

These resins are used for the manufacture of air drying coatings, having durability and mechanical properties normally only associated with high-quality stoving paints. Such coatings may therefore be used on heat-sensitive substrates such as various plastics and in applications where expensive heat curing is not justified. A major area of application is in air drying repair enamels for cars. Available under the trade name Synocure, Cray Valley Products were the first manufacturers in the world of this type of resin.

REPROGRAPHICS DIVISION

The recently established Reprographics Division manufactures toners for the copying industry. Starting with liquid toners for zinc oxide coated papers, our technology has been progressively advanced to keep pace with this fast developing market.

More recently powder toners have commanded an increasing share of the market with the wide use of plain paper copiers and the introduction of powder magnetic toners for use with zinc oxide papers. Having developed a range of these toners, close co-operation with major international manufacturers of machines is progressing towards the development of the potentially simpler and more efficient magnetic toner systems for use in the next generation of plain paper copiers.

Research and development is continuous in order to meet the demands of a technology associated with the growing need for improved communications.

LITHOGRAPHIC PLATES DIVISION

This division was the first and is still the only manufacturer of multimetal plates in the United Kingdom, and is one of three other such manufacturers in Europe. These plates, sold under the trade name Nuchrome, are by universal acclaim the most trouble free and durable lithographic plate. However, the future role of this plate in the lithographic industry is still in doubt, in view of its greater initial cost than surface aluminum plates.

1

SERVE THE PRINTING WORLD
2

3

Changing tastes and changing times:
typical Coates trademarks from (1) the 1930s and 1940s, (2) the 1950s, and (3) today's.

79

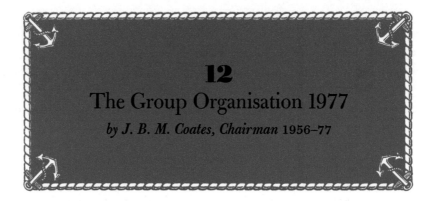

This centenary year of 1977 provides in itself a fitting occasion on which to review the current position of the Coates Group of Companies; but the occasion is made the more fitting since in terms of personalities as well as of years 1977 marks the end of an era. I, myself, retired as Group Chairman in October 1977 and will retire as a director at 31 December 1977. Five other directors, all of whom have played a major part in building the company during the last 40 years, have also recently retired: Charlie Fox, Chief Accountant, Financial Controller and Financial Director (1971); Lance Coates, Laboratory Manager, Technical Director, Export Manager and Deputy Chairman (1975); Andrew Ruck, Technical Director and Deputy Chairman (1976); Robin Nunneley, Assistant General Manager, Joint Managing Director and Deputy Chairman (1976); Tony Harrison, Works Chemist, Works Manager, Production Controller and Production Director (1976).

The first two directors played a large part in the company's renaissance and expansion during the pre-war years. Andrew Ruck and Tony Harrison joined the company immediately after the war and Robin Nunneley joined in 1956. Without these people, all so different in their temperament and ability, Coates, as we know it today, would not be the same. I should mention also three others who played a major part throughout the post-war period in developing the organisation: Jack Tremain joined us in 1945 as Managing Director of Cray Valley Products Ltd, then a small and unknown company. Under his guidance and with the help of Andrew Ruck and Graham North on the technical side together with Tony Harrison on the production side, this company grew within a period of thirty years, until it became a technical leader and major producer of surface coatings and synthetic resins. Jim Cropper, Chairman of Coates Brothers (New Zealand) Ltd and Managing Director of Neill Cropper & Co. Ltd, from whom the original company was purchased, died of a heart attack in 1976 at the early age of 60. Those who worked with him for many years, and especially, Roger Manuel, will know that he was always more than a non-

EXECUTIVE DIRECTORS OF COATES BROTHERS & COMPANY LTD
BEFORE THEIR RETIREMENT

C. C. Fox 1933–71

A. D. A. Ruck 1946–76

R. M. C. Nunneley 1956–76

A. A. Harrison 1946–76

A. Tremain, Managing Director and subsequently Chairman of Cray Valley Products Ltd 1946–76

H. D. A. Heesom, Managing Director of Coates Brothers (South Africa) Ltd 1936–66; Chairman of Coates Brothers (South Africa) Ltd 1966–76

executive chairman and took a great interest in guiding the company's development during all stages of its growth.

Likewise Owen Ellison, Chairman of the Australian company from its inception until he retired in December 1974, and one of the ablest lawyers in Australia, was of immense help to everyone, especially during the early and formative years of the Australian company. The Australian company was fortunate indeed to enjoy the wise leadership of such a man – and one with his wide outside interests as a leading breeder of racehorses, as well as in the financial world – for 25 years.

Finally, Denys Heesom, who was appointed Managing Director of the South African company when it was first established in 1936, retired after 43 years service in October 1976. He was appointed Chairman in 1965, but resigned as Managing Director in 1966 as a result of ill health remaining as Chairman.

With the rapid growth of the company from the mid 1950s onwards, new forms of organisation were of paramount importance. I will not relate details of the evolution of today's organisation, but a brief description of the management structure today (1977) both by companies and by divisions, may be of interest. A chart on page 95 shows the organisation of the group by companies and lists the principal factories. The chart on pages 96–7 describes the UK organisation by divisions and group services function. The underlying purpose behind this organisation is to implement the principles of specialisation and decentralisation referred to in my preface. The most important principle behind this UK organisation is divisional autonomy in all management matters other than those provided by group services. The chief executives of the different divisions, as at October 1977, are as follows:

Division	Selling Company	Chief Executive
Synthetic Resins	Cray Valley Products Ltd	A. G. North, *Managing Director*
Printing Inks	Coates Brothers Inks Ltd Malcolm Wade & Co. Ltd Coates Brothers Inks (Scotland) Ltd Coates of Ireland Ltd	J. P. Walters *Managing Director*
Finishes Division	Coates Brothers Industrial Finishes Ltd	Dr J. B. Ley *Managing Director*
Reprographics Division	Coates Brothers Reprographics Ltd	P. B. Thompson, *General Manager*
Litho Plates and Chemicals Division	Coates Brothers Litho Plates Ltd	J. M. Brown *General Manager*
Overseas Division	Various overseas companies	J. B. Darroch *Overseas Director* J. D. Jackson *Overseas Manager*
Europe and Export Division (E & E)	Coates Brothers (Europe & Export) Ltd	R. B. Howie *General Manager* E. N. Heesom *Assistant General Manager*

The development of this organisation, with each division managed by an experienced executive fully familiar with the technological and commercial aspects of the products concerned, has been of immense help in simplifying the management of the company, both in the UK and overseas. Heading up this team are Sir Richard Meyjes, Deputy Chairman, who succeeded myself as Group Chairman in November 1977, and Ian Meredith who was appointed UK Managing Director in January 1976. I have the greatest confidence that these able executives will continue to lead and guide the company in its further development in the future. We are fortunate indeed to be able to call upon so much ability and experience, following the retirement of the older generation of directors.

Combined with the overseas organisation the Group turnover in 1976 exceeded £75 million. In spite of significant price increases due to inflation, this still reflects a very large increase in comparison with 1947, the first year of public company status, when Group turnover was £1¼ million, or in 1939 when the UK turnover was £224,000 and overseas turnover insignificant. In all the overseas territories the pattern of development has been similar to the UK but with a varying time lag, depending upon the economic circumstances of each territory. Manufacture of printing ink is started initially, with a simple blending operation, usually confined to paste inks. This is gradually extended to include liquid inks and metal coatings products. As the business grows, dry colour manufacturing techniques, the manufacture of oleo resinous vehicles and, in the more advanced companies, synthetic resins, pigmented dispersions of synthetic resins (chips) and reprographic materials are introduced. In the most advanced territories (South Africa and Australia) management structures to operate the divisional and regional organisation first devised in the UK are developed.

None of these changes happen overnight or without very considerable problems of gestation. The selection and development of suitable executives and staff is an art in itself and in many territories it is still necessary to rely upon experts from the home organisation in key technical and financial appointments. Nevertheless, the Group's policy is, in all territories, to recruit and develop indigenous personnel with the appropriate educational qualifications, for whom training within the UK organisation is normally arranged once local recruits of proven calibre have been selected.

I will conclude my remarks on the Group organisation as it is in 1977 with a brief description of the product range manufactured by each division.

Synthetic Resins

Cray Valley Products Ltd is the largest manufacturer of surface coating synthetic resins in the UK and is steadily extending its export of specialised resins to European and other territories. The principal products manufactured are as under:

Alkyd resins for the paint industry

Section of the millroom manufacturing basic intermediates at St Mary Cray factory

Gelkyd (thixotropic) resins for the manufacture of decorative paints and especially 'do it yourself' paints
Polyamide resins for the printing ink, paint and adhesive industries
Acrylic resins for the paint and printing ink industries
Water soluble resins (Resydrol) for the manufacture of industrial finishes
Polyester resins for industrial construction, e.g. boat building

The manufacture, sale and commercial application of these resins is serviced by a large number of chemists and technicians organised into three major sectors as under:

Research and development
Commercial application and service
Testing and control

Printing Ink Division

The manufacture of printing inks for the production of print alone, whether in the form of periodicals, books or commercial illustrations, today represents only

85

a small component of the total production by the industry. To an increasing extent, printing inks have been used as important raw materials in the packaging industry and in many industrial applications. Important examples of end products for which printing inks in one form or another are critical raw materials, are as under:

Newspapers and periodicals
General printing including books, maps, brochures, etc.
Labels and cartons
Printing on film for the flexible packaging industry
Printing on aluminium or tinplate for the rigid container industry
A wide variety of printing for display advertising
Printing on high density polythene for the plastic container industry
Printed circuits and resists for the electronics industry
Printing of heat transfer paper for wet and dry textile transfer processes on different fibres including, especially, polyester, nylon and natural fibres

The formulation and manufacture of printing inks for such diverse purposes can only be undertaken by companies able to deploy large laboratory staffs, to ensure the correct qualities of the products not only as they are delivered but also in their end use applications.

Industrial Finishes

The most important product range manufactured by this division is that of coatings and lacquers for the metal container industry, printing on either tinplate or aluminium. The introduction of new technologies based upon deep drawn cans extruded from a flat metal sheet has created the need for specialised coatings and new methods of decoration. The long testing and proving time required to establish the performance of internal protective lacquers for food and beverage cans and the critical importance of uniformity in the finished product, necessitates extreme care not only in formulation but also in manufacture and quality control. The basis of all these coatings are synthetic resins in one form or another, many of them tailormade for the particular end use application. In the whole group of products manufactured by the surface coatings industry, there is no more critical or difficult group of products to make and control than stoving lacquers and coatings for the metal container industry. It is a great tribute to Dr Ley and his team that the pre-eminence of the company's technology in this area has been established against world competition.

Other products for which coatings and lacquers are manufactured by this division include the following:

Tubes for toothpaste and other specialised products
Decorated cannisters for the paint and other industries

A high-speed gravure press used for printing transfer paper for subsequent sublimation on to the fabric when processed through the transfer print machine shown below

Hunt & Moscop transfer print machine. This machine is used to transfer the design from paper to fabric in the transfer printing process. The paper passes over hot rollers and the dyestuff is 'fixed' to the fabric by sublimation

Decorated tins and containers for a wide variety of industries, such as boot polish, floor polish, etc., biscuit tins, tea caddies, etc.
Decorated drums for the oil industry

Reprographics Division

This new division, under the leadership of Peter Thompson, has within a space of seven years established itself as a world leader in the manufacture of liquid and powder toners for the fast growing copying industry. These materials have to be manufactured to meet critical performance tests based upon the opposite polarity of electric charges, which is the principle underlying the instantaneous production of documents from a wide variety of copying machines, competing against the original Rank Xerox installations. The Japanese machine manufacturers are rapidly challenging the American lead and former monopoly in this industry. Toners are purpose-made for each individual machine and are normally marketed by the machine manufacturer. Continuous

Chemist in Reprographics laboratory, testing out new toners on a Mita Copystar 900 magnetic copier; one of the latest models using magnetic toners for document reproduction on plain paper

technological development by the machine manufacturers and suppliers of special paper, demands an extremely high level of technological achievement by the toner manufacturer, and it is gratifying to observe how the many difficult problems of raw material selection, production and packaging have been tackled and overcome by our technical staffs.

Manufacture of reprographic products, in accordance with specifications produced by the UK division, is now being progressively expanded, in the company's recently established plant in Brussels and in association with our existing overseas companies in South Africa and Australia.

Litho Plates Division

This division manufactures multi-metal litho plates and chemicals for the lithographic industry. It caters for only a small sector of the world market and has experienced considerable difficulties in establishing uniformity of manufacture in what must be one of the most difficult electroplating technologies required for any end use. In spite of the problems steady progress has been achieved, and it is believed that there will be a permanent requirement for this type of plate in view of its high performance and durability.

Overseas Division

As well as providing the technical and managerial advice which is regularly made available to all our overseas manufacturing companies, this division is also responsible for the manufacture and sale to these companies of a wide range of intermediate products made in the company's UK factories as well as raw materials which are neither made in the local territory or within the Group organisation. The importance of this division in promoting the growth and efficiency of the overseas companies through regular visits to each territory and through the reception and training of visitors and local recruits cannot be over-estimated.

E & E Division

This division is a loose agglomeration of various functions which have yet to be properly integrated. It is responsible for direct exports to end users of printing ink and metal coatings products, in territories not serviced by our overseas or European companies. The contracts sector of this division is responsible for the sale of technical know-how and the negotiation of factory projects in territories with state-controlled economies. The division is also responsible for the provision of technical and managerial advice and the supply of raw materials and intermediate products to the Group's subsidiary and associated companies in Europe.

Sir Keith Joseph, Minister of State at the Board of Trade, during a visit to
St Mary Cray factory 16 January 1962

Group Services

Linking together each operating division with central management is the Group
Services Organisation, providing common services for the operational management of each separate division. These services are as under:

Finance and Accounting
Central Purchasing
Personnel and Labour Policy
Legal and Secretarial Services
Construction and Building Maintenance

The Financing and Accounting Organisation, including the computer and
data processing services, is located at St Mary Cray under the control of Peter
Martin as Financial Controller, being responsible, himself, to Joe Darroch,
Financial Director. Apart from the normal requirements of an accounting
organisation, including invoicing, debt collection and payment of creditors, the
financial and accounting sector of Group Services is responsible in addition for
the following:

Monthly trading statements and quarterly accounts for each UK division and European subsidiary company

Monitoring of the cash flow and utilisation of working capital including short term investment

Providing information concerning the rate of expenditure in accordance with the capital expenditure budget

Subject to directions from the main board, negotiation of banking and loan facilities

Through the overseas accountant located at Easton Street, this department is also responsible for co-ordinating and interpreting the financial situation of all overseas companies

The central purchasing organisation, also located at St Mary Cray, is responsible for the purchase of raw materials for all divisions. A subsidiary purchasing function mainly dealing with engineering components is located in South Wales. The chief buyer is Selby Freeman, who joined the company in 1938 and has occupied this position ever since. He is widely respected in the trade where he is regarded as the last of the old style buyers in the oil and colour industries, who has himself an intimate knowledge of the raw materials which he purchases.

The central personnel department and the secretarial department is located at Easton Street. The staff manager, Mr Meadows Smith, is at Easton Street and there are personnel officers located at St Mary Cray and South Wales factories.

Mr Harris-Matthews is the company's secretary and Mr D. J. Youngman is the director responsible for both the secretarial and personnel departments, as well as for the co-ordination of labour policy. Negotiations with the trades unions are handled at industry level through the Society of British Printing Ink Manufacturers and the Chemical Industry Association respectively.

The construction and building maintenance department is located at St Mary Cray factory under the control of the company architect – John Grover. All building expenditure is sanctioned at main board level and building policy generally is under the control of the UK managing director through the production controller and the company architect.

It will be apparent, therefore, that the Group Services Organisation plays an extremely important role in the management of all manufacturing and commercial operations in the home market. Through the overseas accountant it also provides an information service to the main board on the trading performance and current liquidity situation of the overseas companies.

The above review concludes this history of Coates during the last one hundred years. Growth of the company over the period can most conveniently be viewed through a comparison of the sales turnover for different years, although this needs to be related to the changes in the value of money, especially during the last six years. The relevant figures are as under:

Chemist testing liquid inks for printing on film
on a Moser flexo/gravure experimental press in
the development laboratories at St Mary Cray
factory

Date	Sales turnover in £ sterling	Approximate degree of inflation since previous date	Remarks
1890	£15,000	—	Private limited company established in 1889
1914	£30,586	Nil	Start of World War I
1929	£75,019	64%	Death of George Coates one of the founders
1939	£224,449	Nil	Start of World War II
1948	£1,252,000	94%	Public company status obtained
1970	£22,822,000*	116%	John Coates retires as Managing Director remaining as Chairman
1976	£75,329,000*	115%	Three executive directors retire at 31 December

*Consolidated Group figures

The whole of the company's substantial growth since the war, with the
exception of the £200,000 of preference capital required to start the South

Wales factory, has been financed out of retained earnings and short-term bank finance. It has been an essential part of the directors' philosophy to develop through innovation and internal initiative rather than through external acquisition. A number of relatively small acquisitions have been made but the difficulties of integrating a company with a different management philosophy and technical management should never be underestimated; thus it is that the most successful acquisitions have been those with a useful factory on to which can be superimposed, without management problems, the company's own production and commercial methods.

And now what of the future? This poses a big question mark, not because of the company and its ability, for I really believe that for Coates there is a great and growing part which, in ordinary circumstances, it could look forward to playing as one of the leading companies in the world in its own fields; but in Britain, at any rate, these are by no means ordinary times. On a global basis there is a clash of ideologies between the ideas personified by America in the western world and the dogma personified by Russia in much of Asia and Eastern Europe. It seems probable to me that there will be no resolution of these very different ideologies for a long time and that attempts by each to influence the so-called third world countries to their way of thinking, will continue. In Britain, however, a special situation seems to have developed, analagous with the circumstances before the Civil War in the 17th century. As a result it is no longer possible to take for granted a gradual development in the future, on a basis of continuity with the past, subject to adaptation to slowly changing ideas and economic circumstances.

Every organisation has within it the seeds of organic growth or decay, according to the quality of its leadership and achievement. Most people at Coates would like to see the company remain independent; and indeed, without independence, its status, as all of us have known it, will inevitably change or even be destroyed completely. But if, in fact, a major discontinuity develops within the British environment, the prospects of survival will be conditioned, in the main, by political developments over which few people have any control at all, least of all those who have laboured for many years to promote the discontinuity.

And so it is that the future leadership of Coates may find it hard to continue the tradition of nearly all successful industrialists hitherto, that of avoiding political choice. I, myself, am still hopeful that this dilemma will not arise; but if it does (and this could happen, perhaps, quite soon), I feel confident that the choice will be made in favour of maintaining, as far as is practicable, the independence and quality of the organisation and its achievement, without which there is no satisfaction either for those who work within the company or for those who rely upon its products and service for their own particular purposes.

I will therefore end by returning once again to the beginning, and expressing my firmly-held belief, that all progress through generations, amid the differing views of so many people, must depend in the ultimate on faith: to survive and to meet the challenge of changing circumstances each must have faith in himself, in those around him and in their ability to safeguard the future of his own country.

Coates Brothers & Company Limited
Organisation by companies

BRITISH AND IRISH COMPANIES
Coates Brothers Inks Ltd
Coates Brothers Inks Scotland Ltd
Coates of Ireland Ltd
Malcolm Wade & Co. Ltd
Cray Valley Products Ltd
Coates Brothers Industrial Finishes Ltd
Coates Brothers Litho Plates Ltd
Coates Brothers Reprographics Ltd

EUROPEAN COMPANIES
Vendelboe A/S
Coates France S.A.
Cray Valley Products S.A.
S.A. Cray Valley Products N.V.
S.A. Coates N.V.
A/S Drubin*
Prisma S.A.*

OVERSEAS COMPANIES
Coates Brothers (South Africa) Ltd
Cray Valley Products S.A. Pty Ltd
Coates Brothers (Central Africa) Pvt Ltd
Coates Brothers (Zambia) Ltd
Coates Brothers (East Africa) Ltd
Coates Brothers (West Africa) Ltd
Coates Brothers (Jamaica) Ltd
Coates Brothers (Caribbean) Ltd
Coates Brothers Australia Pty Ltd
Coates Brothers (New Zealand) Ltd
Coates of India Ltd
Coates Brothers (Singapore) Pte Ltd
Coates Brothers (Malaysia) Ltd
P.T. Coates – Indonesia
Coates Brothers (Hong Kong) Ltd

Associate Companies

COATES BROTHERS & COMPANY LIMITED
UNITED KINGDOM ORGANISATION
GROUP HEADQUARTERS

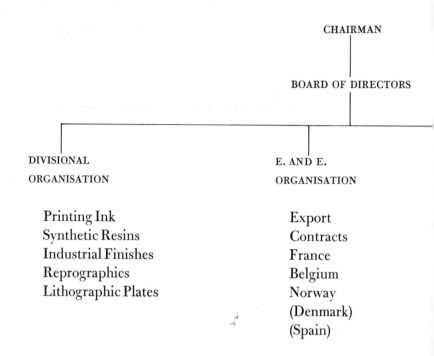

CHAIRMAN

BOARD OF DIRECTORS

DIVISIONAL
ORGANISATION

Printing Ink
Synthetic Resins
Industrial Finishes
Reprographics
Lithographic Plates

E. AND E.
ORGANISATION

Export
Contracts
France
Belgium
Norway
(Denmark)
(Spain)

BASIC FACTORIES

Sidcup, Kent	*Industrial finishes*
St. Mary Cray, Kent	*Printing ink – two factories*
Machen, Gwent (South Wales)	*Synthetic resins; finishes; litho plates*
Stallingborough, Lincolnshire	*Synthetic resins*
Midsomer Norton, Somerset	*Printing ink; reprographics*

May 1977

GROUP SERVICES
ORGANISATION

    Finance and Accounts
    Secretarial and Legal
    Personnel and Labour
    Central Purchasing
    Building and Construction

OVERSEAS
ORGANISATION

    London Headquarters
    Australia
    New Zealand
    Singapore
    Hong Kong
    Malaysia
    India
    South Africa
    Rhodesia
    Zambia
    Kenya
    Nigeria
    Jamaica
    Trinidad

BRANCH FACTORIES OF THE
PRINTING INK DIVISION

Glasgow
Belfast
Newcastle
Leeds
Manchester
Birmingham
Nottingham
St. Mary Cray
Midsomer Norton

COATES BROTHERS & COMPANY LIMITED

Sales Turnover 1877–1950

	£		£
1877	2,327	1914	30,586
1878	4,658	1915	30,462
1879	5,481	1916	42,286
1880	8,573	1917	38,329
1881	12,000+	1918	43,717
1882	Missing	1919	44,341
1883	Missing	1920	67,685
1884	Missing	1921	40,876
1885	Missing	1922	48,502
1886	14,147	1923	52,116
1887	13,457	1924	59,711
1888	13,657	1925	64,751
1889	13,725	1926	64,433
1890	13,772	1927	64,005
1891	13,475	1928	70,649
1892	15,392	1929	75,019
1893	17,408	1930	78,580
1894	17,876	1931	87,724
1895	18,505	1932	96,639
1896	19,686	1933	113,053
1897	22,244	1934	135,906
1898	21,293	1935	155,154
1899	22,540	1936	172,652
1900	22,784	1937	203,548
1901	18,837	1938	205,381
1902	19,356	1939	224,449
1903	18,522	1940	213,058
1904	19,392	1941	268,443
1905	20,467	1942	320,981
1906	21,115	1943	Missing
1907	22,308	1944	Missing
1908	22,958	1945	Missing
1909	22,751	1946	Missing
1910	26,359	1947	1,056,488
1911	27,770	1948	1,012,520
1912	28,072	1949	884,541
1913	28,534	1950	1,158,802

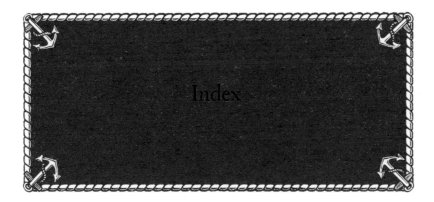

Index

100